The Book of
Secrets

THE BOOK OF
Secrets

The Way to Wealth and Success

A Fable

ROBERT J. PETRO

AND

THERESE A. FINCH

HarperSanFrancisco
An Imprint of HarperCollins*Publishers*

To my wife, Marlena, for her love and support

R.F.

To my parents, George and Josephine Fakoury, and
to my husband, Gregory, for his help and encouragement

T.F.

A TREE CLAUSE BOOK

HarperSanFrancisco and the authors, in association with The Basic
Foundation, a not-for-profit organization whose primary mission is
reforestation, will facilitate the planting of two trees for every one
tree used in the manufacture of this book.

HarperCollins Web Site: http://www.harpercollins.com

HarperCollins®, 📖 ®, HarperSanFrancisco™, and A TREE CLAUSE
BOOK are trademarks of HarperCollins Publishers Inc.

FIRST EDITION

Library of Congress Cataloging-in-Publication Data

Petro, Robert J.
    The book of secrets : the way to wealth and success /
  Robert J. Petro and Therese A. Finch. —1st ed.
    ISBN 0–06–251478–4 (cloth)
    ISBN 0–06–251497–0 (pbk.)
    ISBN 0–06–251515–2 (intl.)
      I. Finch, Therese A. II. Title.
PS3566.E83B66   1997
813'.54—dc21   96–47659

99 00 01 ❖ RRD(H) 10 9 8 7 6 5 4 3 2

Contents

The Legacy

NTONIO JUMPED OUT OF BED AND LOOKED OUT
the window. It was almost light. He dressed and
raced downstairs. "Morning, Miguel," he said to the
cook. "Is Grandpa up yet?"

Miguel nodded. "He's out saddling the horses. How about
some breakfast?"

"I'm not hungry." Antonio ran out the back door and
headed straight for the barn. "Grandpa, you out here?" he
called.

Juan Gomez broke into a big grin when he saw his only
grandchild. "How's my favorite grandson this morning?"

"Just fine." Antonio returned his grandfather's smile.
"How's my favorite grandpa?"

Their eyes met for an endearing second. Though they
went through this ritual every morning, neither of them
seemed to tire of it. Juan put his arm around Antonio. "You
ready to go?"

"I'm so excited, Grandpa. We haven't done this . . . since
Papa . . ."

"I know, I know," Juan said reassuringly. "I'm sorry I've
neglected you lately. Running this estate alone takes so much
time."

"But today, it's just you and me—right Grandpa?"
Antonio said.

"Right," Grandpa said, mussing Antonio's hair. "Now go
get that picnic lunch Miguel packed for us."

As soon as Antonio was out of sight, Juan Gomez doubled
over. Leaning against the barn door, he held his breath until
the stabbing pain in his left arm subsided.

In the kitchen, Miguel said to Antonio, "There's juice in the alcove."

"Oh, okay," Antonio said, and walked into the sunroom. Anna smiled at him.

"Hi Mom." Antonio kissed her cheek. Then, picking up the juice, he gulped it down. "Gotta go," he said. "Grandpa's waiting."

"Have fun," she called after her son, happy to see him in such high spirits.

Juan and Antonio began riding to the southern end of the estate. "You know, Antonio, someday I hope all this will be yours."

"Me too, Grandpa. You taught me to love the land. Now will you teach me how to run it?"

"When the time is right," Juan said, his eyes shining with pride.

"I think I'm ready."

"Perhaps so. You're so much wiser than I was at your age."

"Did your father teach you?" Antonio assumed that his grandpa had lived on the estate all his life, just as he and Anna had.

"No," Juan said. "My growing up was not quite as easy as yours."

"How so, Grandpa? You always promised to tell me that story. We have time now, don't we?"

Pausing briefly, Juan whispered, "Maybe."

Antonio shot a glance at his slumping grandfather. "What's the matter, Grandpa?"

"Help me," Juan said, feebly.

Jumping off of his horse, Antonio eased the old man down.

"It's hot," Juan said. "So hot."

Trying to conceal the alarm rising in his voice, Antonio said, "Grandpa, it's cool this morning, just the way you like it." He half-dragged the pale man to a shady spot under a tree. "I'm going to get help."

Juan lightly touched the boy's arm. "No. Wait," he said. "We must talk."

"You need a doctor. We can talk later."

"There may not be time." Juan took a sip of the water Antonio offered. "After I'm gone," Juan continued, "you may think I deserted you. Truth is, I've tried to protect you and your mother."

Antonio's eyes brimmed with tears. "What are you talking about, Grandpa?"

"I had no choice, son." Juan's voice sounded labored. "Just have faith and remember, I'll always be with you."

Confused and frightened, Antonio jumped on his horse and galloped back to the house. "Mama, Mama," he yelled. "Grandpa passed out down by the caves."

Glancing at Miguel, Anna said, "Send for the doctor. I'll take a couple of men and go get him."

But they were too late. Juan Gomez was dead.

On the morning of the funeral, Antonio awoke early. He looked out his window and saw the empty, waiting caisson. That thing was taking his grandpa away forever. He shivered. First Papa, now Grandpa. He was the man of the house. And he had no idea what to do.

Antonio dressed slowly. He dreaded Grandpa's remains leaving the house. It was so final. Even dead, the body somehow provided comfort.

Antonio crept downstairs. He thought about that last morning, how excited he'd been to finally have an outing with Grandpa again. Entering the kitchen, he was surprised to see the cooks bustling about. "Miguel," he asked. "What's going on?"

Miguel rolled his eyes heavenward. "We're having four hundred for dinner tonight."

"Tonight? But why?"

"It was his wish. In the forty years I've known that man . . . this is the craziest . . . a big celebration after the reading."

Antonio didn't ask what Miguel meant by a reading. All he could focus on was Grandpa's imminent funeral.

After making some hot chocolate, Antonio walked into the sunlit alcove. For a blinding moment, he found reassurance in the light and warmth. Then, he saw Anna. He bent down to kiss her wet cheek. "Good morning, Mama," he said.

Anna's eyes were red and swollen. "I'm going to miss him so much."

"Me, too," Antonio said. "I shouldn't have left him that day. It's all my fault he's dead."

"No, my heart," she said. "Grandpa hadn't been well for some time. He didn't want us to know."

"Why not? Maybe we could have helped."

"I don't think so. The doctor said it was just a matter of time."

"I'm scared, Mama. What's going to happen to us?"

Anna closed her eyes, her breath stuttering in. "Have faith. It will all work out, you'll see."

Just then Miguel came in. "It's almost time," he said.

Anna nodded. "Are you set for tonight?"

"Not quite. But we can discuss it later."

Anna turned to Antonio, emotion filling her face. "I'm going to get ready."

A little while later, Antonio walked into the living room. He ran his hand along the edge of the huge mahogany casket. His heart ached so. "Good-bye, Grandpa," he whispered, a tear trickling down his cheek. "I'm going to miss you."

The funeral took place in a village near the ranch, not far from Mexico City. The church was filled to overflowing. Following the casket in, Antonio and Anna nodded to the many mourners. These people are going to miss Grandpa's fairness and honesty, Antonio thought, but I'm going to miss his love.

After the service, about fifty followed the caisson to the cemetery. Everyone except Anna and Antonio left after the priest said benediction. They stayed while the casket was lowered into the ground. Still in shock, they watched as the first piles of dirt hit the shiny brown box.

"Let's go, Mama," Antonio said, squeezing her hand.

Anna lingered a little while before nodding her ascent.

Inside the carriage, they sat in silence while the buggy bumped along the dirt road. Anna sniffed, occasionally dabbing at her eyes. Finally, she spoke. "Sandoval is reading the will at eleven," she said. "He wants you there too."

"Me? Why?"

"I guess Papa left you something."

"I don't understand any of this," Antonio said, distraught. "He promised he'd always be with me and now he's gone."

"I'm sorry he promised you that, my darling." Anna put her arm around Antonio, "No one can guarantee life will continue."

When they arrived home, the mansion was filled with the same men Antonio had seen at the funeral. For a fleeting moment, he wondered why the hired hands were there.

But once he had made it through the crowd and upstairs, he forgot all about them. In his room, a picture of Juan Gomez as a young man distracted him. How little he knew of Grandpa's life then. He felt sad that they hadn't had more time.

Suddenly, Antonio smiled. The resemblance between his grandfather and him was remarkable. Grandpa's face always lit up when people called Antonio the Junior Juan.

At exactly eleven o'clock, Antonio walked into the library. Sandoval, the lawyer, closed the heavy wooden doors, settled into Grandpa's chair, and pulled a thick pile of papers from his briefcase. A hush fell over the room.

Somberly, Sandoval began to read, "I, Juan Gomez, being of sound mind and body, do hereby bequeath the following . . ."

Antonio listened with a pounding heart. He knew and loved every inch of the estate. So he realized immediately that Grandpa was parceling it and doling it out to his loyal ranch hands and his household staff.

Why? Antonio paled. Grandpa had promised him the land. He looked over at his mother. She sat rigid, her hands folded in her lap, her eyes passive.

Antonio rubbed his forehead. I thought he loved us. Then Grandpa's words, "You may think I deserted you," echoed in his head. It was difficult to feel otherwise. Grandpa promised he'd always be with him, too. Yet he and his mom were alone.

The penultimate bequest went to Anna. Grandpa left her the Victorian, the fifty acres surrounding it, the house in Mexico City, and quite a sum of cash.

Finally, Antonio heard, "Lastly, I bequeath to my grandson, Antonio, my greatest legacy." Confused, Antonio wondered what that could be. The land was gone, stripped out from under him.

In a daze, Antonio approached the huge desk as Sandoval pulled a wooden box out of a drawer. The box reminded him of Grandpa's casket. Blinking back tears, he accepted the keepsake and the old-fashioned key that went with it.

Antonio clutched the gift to his heart and rushed out of the library, his head lowered. In his room, he sank down on the bed and, with a trembling hand, placed the key into the lock.

Opportunity Is Everywhere

A NXIOUS, ANTONIO LIFTED THE COVER. HE STARED in disbelief. There must be some mistake. Flipping through the contents, he saw only a bunch of papers. Surely, Grandpa would have left him more. Maybe Sandoval misunderstood.

Tears filled his eyes. His heart ached so. Overcome with grief, he sobbed into his pillow.

A while later, he rolled onto his back and stared at the ceiling, emotionally drained. As he mulled over the last few days, Grandpa's words kept running through his mind. "You will think I've deserted you, but I will always be with you." What was Grandpa trying to tell him? Was there a message in the box?

Antonio sat up. This time he saw a letter addressed to him:

My Dearest Antonio:

Since you're reading this, my worst fears have happened. I have died and left you and your mom all alone. I'm sorry, little one. I know what it's like to be cast adrift without an anchor.

I had suspected for some time that I was ill. When Dr. Quintana told me to get my affairs in order, I started writing this journal, my Book of Secrets, for you.

My task consumed me. I was so scared my heart would give out before completing it. When I felt good, I'd scoff at my obsession, believing I'd live to see you become a man. But life doesn't always bestow what we think we deserve. At least now I can rest easy knowing it is finished.

More than anything, I wanted you to have the estate. But the civil war is under way; the rebel forces are rising up and violently taking our land. With news of my death, they would have made our home a prime target. Hopefully, I've saved you and your mother a lot of political turmoil.

I know you don't feel it now, but nothing is lost. And you are not alone. These pages contain all the knowledge you'll ever need to succeed in this world. These secrets of success, these lessons for living well, studied and practiced, will guide you into manhood. I hope you'll learn as I did that money is only one aspect of true wealth.

My dear Antonio, even though I'm gone now, my spirit lives on within these pages. It is through them that I have indeed left you my true fortune.

All my love,

Grandpa

For the first time since Grandpa died, Antonio felt comforted. Grabbing a stack of papers, he settled back on his pillows and continued reading.

∼ BOOK OF SECRETS

I grew up on a *rancheria* about fifteen miles southwest of Pachuca. When I was seventeen, my parents died—my mom in January and my dad in May. I had no other family.

My neighbors took pity on me and offered to let me stay with them. But they were poor and couldn't support me. I did accept their help planting the corn, however. After a long, hard workday, I returned home for my first night alone.

The memories in that two-room hut hung like a choker around my neck. When I couldn't stand it anymore, I took my straw mat out to the barn to stay with my donkey and best friend, Teresa.

When I saw Teresa, I squeezed her so tight I thought I was going to break her neck. It felt good just to be near a warm body. "Hope you don't mind sharing tonight, girl. I don't want to be alone."

Teresa continued eating, but she swished her tail long enough to let me know I was welcomed.

"I'm scared, girl," I said, my teeth chattering. "The corn is planted, but how can I grow a crop by myself?"

Teresa licked my face as if to say we'll make it.

"You're the only one who understands how lost I feel." I started pacing. "You know Dad ran everything. He never gave me any responsibility. Now I have to do it myself. I don't even know where to begin."

Teresa watched me pace. "Okay. Okay," I said. "So that's not entirely true. But . . . damn this farm. There's always so much to do. That's what killed him. That's what killed both of them."

With each pass, my frenzy grew. Teresa plodded across the barn and settled down alongside my mat and waited for me.

Finally, I joined her. "Sorry, girl. I just don't know what to do."

Teresa gently muzzled me back on my mat. With her warm body next to mine, I eventually relaxed and fell asleep. It was just before dawn.

Several hours later, Teresa nudged me awake. She seemed unsettled and soon I heard why. A horse-drawn cart came clacking up the path. I peeked through the crack in the door, and gulped when I saw the landlord heading toward the house.

"Señor Hernandez," I said, opening the barn door. "What brings you out here this fine morning?"

Hernandez took off his hat, wiping the dust off his brow. "I was sorry to hear about your father."

He didn't come all this way just to offer condolences. "Señor, you'd be proud," I said, attempting to sound upbeat. "The fields are planted."

Hernandez looked surprised. "But . . . how?"

"The neighbors helped. We finished yesterday."

Hernandez stared past me. "That's all well and good," he said. "But you can't produce a crop all by yourself." He shuffled his feet. "I've already arranged for some new tenants to move in. They arrive the day after tomorrow."

"You can't do that. This is my home."

"I'm sorry, Juan," he said, putting on his hat. "I have no choice."

Hot tears stung my eyes. "Farming's all I know, Señor. Please . . . let me stay."

"Maybe the new tenants can use an extra hand. You ask them."

"And if they don't, what am I to do?"

"I don't know." He turned to leave. "Go to Mexico City. I'm sure you can find something there."

"But Señor," I persisted. "My parents worked for you for twenty years. Is this the thanks they get?"

Reaching into his pocket, Hernandez tossed some pesos into the dirt. "There. That should make us even." Then he climbed into his wagon, picked up the reins, and said, "I want you off my land tomorrow."

Stunned, I watched him until he turned into a speck of dust. Then I gathered his paltry offering and walked into the house. I spent the day sorting through personal items. Later, in the setting sun, I took my last tour of the farm. Most of my life had been tilled into this soil. Now my parents were gone and soon I would be too.

I again spent the night in the barn. When I saw Teresa, I bit back the tears. "It's so unfair," I said. "Why should one person have so much power? He snaps his fingers and you're homeless."

I kicked an old milk can, thinking it was empty. The pain shot up my leg. I started to scream. "I hate you, Hernandez, I hate you, I hate you." I held my throbbing toes and hopped around on one foot. "I hate you, father. Why did you leave me alone?"

Sobbing, I fell into a heap on my mat.

Teresa calmed me down by nuzzling the back of my neck. Eventually, I fell into an exhausted sleep.

The next morning, I made my decision. I stuffed most of my personal belongings into two huge saddlebags and loaded them on Teresa. Then I took one long, last look at the house.

Finally, wiping my tears, I started my sixty-some-mile journey to Mexico City.

That day, I walked ten miles. My toes hurt and my shoes were so worn that I felt every pebble in the rocky, potholed road. Because the route was vaguely defined, I lost my way several times and had to backtrack.

After retracing my steps a third time, I sat down atop a hill in some shade to sip some water. I didn't dare drink too much because I hadn't seen a place all day to fill my canteen.

It felt so good to rest that I decided to camp there. After some searching, I found a fairly flat spot a ways from the road. I gathered mesquite twigs and built a fire.

Then, while the stars dotted the darkening sky, I ate a dry tortilla. Hardly enough to fill my empty stomach. Tired and hungry, I fell into a restless sleep.

Several hours later, Teresa nudged me awake. "What's the matter, girl?" I said, patting her neck.

Shortly after, I realized what was troubling her. I heard hooves and voices on the path. Scared, I ran deeper into the scrub. My father refused to travel at night because he believed bandits lurked in the countryside. I didn't know if he was right or wrong, but I wasn't taking any chances.

The men stopped on the crest. I couldn't quite make out what they were saying, but they were excited about something.

What if they smelled my campfire and were looking for me? I prayed they would move on.

Although I heard them gallop off later, I stayed crouched behind a boulder, wondering if they would return. Finally, when Teresa came looking for me, I knew for sure they had gone. "Thanks, girl," I said. "What would I do without you?"

After that, even with Teresa protecting me, I couldn't go back to sleep. I lay there with my eyes wide open, rigid and cold, listening to the night creatures rustle in the underbrush.

At dawn, I got up. "Damn Hernandez," I said to Teresa, loading her back. "He rides around in that cart of his, never getting his hands dirty. Who does he think he is anyway?"

We started on our way. My head buzzed from lack of sleep. Leaning on Teresa, I swore I'd get even with him.

It was hot. We walked for hours, only briefly taking refuge in the shade of the scrub. I'd been unsuccessful in finding water and my canteen was almost empty.

I was about to quit for the day when I spotted a small trail branching from the road. Hoping to find a stream and a safe place to sleep, I followed it into the trees.

But the forest wasn't as thick as I thought and I soon came to a clearing. Across the road was a well-maintained white-washed fence that stretched as far as my eyes could see. I continued walking. The air was utterly still. Suddenly I came upon a magnificent house. My heart quickened. Was I dreaming or did someone really live there?

Weak from hunger and thirst, I pressed on, the rhythmic beat of Teresa's gait pounding the packed dirt. Then I spotted a man stooped over, working in a bed of marigolds.

"Excuse me, Señor," I said, leaning on the fence. "Could I trouble you for some water? We're very thirsty."

The man straightened up. He was dressed rather shabbily. His pants had holes in the knees and his straw hat looked like someone had taken a bite out of it. Must be the gardener, I thought.

He walked toward me. He was wiry, not much taller than my five feet, eight inches, with arms that looked a tad too long for his body. His skin was bronzed, not reddish-brown like mine, and his graying hair hung in sweat-soaked strands under his hat. "You look like you need more than water," he said. "How long you been traveling?"

"Two days, Señor," I said, looking into his sky-blue eyes.

He opened the gate. "There's a well in back. Take as much as you need."

"Thank you," I said. "We'll only be a minute. I want to find a place to sleep before it gets dark."

"You're welcome to the barn."

"I am?" I said. I wondered if I could sleep in the shadow of such a grand place. "Won't the owner mind?"

The man laughed and pointed to the well. "Wash up," he said. "I'll tell the cook to fix you something to eat."

My stomach growled. I was hungrier than I think I'd been in my whole life. "That's very kind of you, Señor, but I don't want to trouble you."

"It's no trouble. No trouble at all," he said, striding toward the house.

I stared after him. Could I really be this lucky? Water, food, a roof over my head. "We better hurry and use the water," I said, pulling Teresa, "because when the owner finds out we're here, he'll kick us out just like Hernandez did."

I splashed water on my face and gave Teresa a long drink. But no one came. So I led my donkey into the huge barn. It felt safe. I hoped we'd be able to stay the night.

Approaching the house, I saw the gardener seated on the back patio at a table set for two. He had changed his clothes and combed his hair. Under the light of the lantern, his face seemed softer—less angular—his nose not quite so prominent and his blue eyes piercing.

I stopped at the base of the step, not wanting to intrude.

"Come here," he said.

I knitted my brow. "You mean sit at the table—with you?"

"Of course," he said. The man no longer looked like a servant. He smiled broadly and the weathered lines around his eyes disappeared into soft crinkles.

I hesitated. "Who are you, anyway?"

"Hector Ortega," he said, "the owner of this place."

I stared at him. "You did all this for me?" Why would someone so rich bother with a poor boy?

"Why not? You looked so tired and hungry. What's your name, young man?"

"Juan Gomez," I said, shaking his outstretched hand.

As soon as I sat down, Miguel, the cook, magically appeared with a plate of hot quesadillas.

"Help yourself," Hector said.

My stomach started contracting. I took one. It felt warm and crisp from frying in the lard. Before setting it down on my plate, I stole a bite. Guacamole, beef, beans, potatoes, cheese, and rice filled my mouth.

Gobbling the first, I tore into the second, then the third, like a hungry dog.

Halfway through my third one, Hector said, "Would you like some more?"

"Thank you, Señor. My stomach feels very empty."

Hector threw back his head and laughed. "Miguel!" he said. "How about a few more for my friend here."

I closed my eyes and savored my last morsel. It was unbelievable, not just food, but great food, just for the asking. Hector hadn't even finished his first. "You don't eat very much, do you?"

"Not as much as I used to," Hector answered, taking a bite with his fork. "My appetite has decreased with age."

Miguel brought out my fourth helping and I ate it at a more civilized pace. Self-consciously, I picked up my fork and started imitating Hector.

"Where're you from?" Hector asked.

"Pachuca, but I'm moving to Mexico City to seek my fortune."

"Is that right?" Hector said. "And what about your parents? Don't they need you at home?"

The mention of my parents made me feel uneasy. "This is quite a place you have here."

"I modeled it after the Victorians in San Francisco."

"Are they as colorful?"

"Oh yes," Hector said, his eyes lighting up.

"I'd like to see them someday."

"I hope you will." Hector wiped his mouth with his napkin. "I'm curious. Why did you leave your home?"

I closed my eyes and took a deep breath. "I don't have a home, thanks to Señor Hernandez."

"Señor Hernandez?"

"Yes, he kicked me off my land. Someday, I'm gonna be rich like him, and I'm going to buy him out."

"What happened to your parents?"

I sipped my drink. Talking about them was too painful. "This is good, what is it?"

"Chicha. It's made from chia seeds." Hector hammered away. "Do your parents know what you're doing?"

"My parents are dead," I said, finally. "I'm all alone."

Just then, Miguel waddled out to serve tea. He was about my age, but had coal black eyes and a bulging stomach. I lowered my head to hide my tears.

An uncomfortable silence hung in the air. Only the sound of Hector stirring sugar into his tea disturbed the quiet. "I'm sorry about your parents," he said gently. "You must have loved them very much."

I swallowed hard and nodded. "My parents wanted something better for me. They assumed many of my chores so I could study."

Hector sipped his tea, watching me.

"They should have let me do my share. It was too stressful on them. If it weren't for me . . ."

"If it weren't for you, what? They wouldn't have died? You can't blame yourself for that. What they did, they did out of love for you."

"Maybe," I said. "But they never had time for me. They never taught me how to survive in the world."

"You'll do fine," Hector said. "I know it's hard to be alone."

I snorted. "What would you know about it?"

"Juan, this wasn't handed to me. I, too, grew up poor. But fear of poverty drove me constantly, until one day I woke up to find I was an old man who had nothing but his money and his land."

"Señor," I said, "I'd gladly change places with you. I am alone with no money."

Hector threw back his head and laughed. "Forgive me for laughing," he said. "It's just that . . . well . . . someday, you'll understand."

"Understand what?"

"It's hard to explain. Age and experience are very good teachers."

I stared at him blankly.

"You must be tired," he said. "Forgive me for keeping you up so late."

After Hector went in, I sat staring at the stars. With my hunger resolved, I felt at peace. What a nice man, I thought. I felt honored that he had spent time with me, a poor boy. I looked down at my tattered clothes and felt embarrassed. Oh well, tomorrow I'll leave and never see him again.

I thought about my parents and felt miserably alone. So I went to get Teresa. She always gave me comfort. With a full stomach and a warm body next to me, I soon fell fast asleep.

The next morning, Hector woke me up. "Good morning," he said. "Breakfast is almost ready."

I washed up and met Hector at the same table as the night before. He watched me eat another three helpings in silence.

Finally, Hector said, "You know, Juan, you remind me a lot of myself at your age. And because of that, I'll tell you something to help you along your way."

My heart pounded wildly. I leaned forward on my elbows, giving Hector my full attention.

"If you look, you'll find opportunity is everywhere. The wise man learns to recognize and seize opportunity any time and any place it is found."

I waited for Hector to say more, but he didn't. "I don't understand," I said.

Hector smiled and patted my hand. "It's getting late, you better get going." He walked me to the gate. "There's a fork in the road about sixteen miles from here. If you follow it west, you'll come to Sanchez's farm. Tell him I sent you, he'll let you spend the night in his barn."

I figured Sanchez's was about four miles from the city. If I left his place early enough, I could get there in time to find a job and a place to sleep. "Thanks for everything," I said. "Especially the food."

"Juan," Hector said, shaking my hand. "I'd like to know what happens to you. Do come back and visit me sometime."

I promised I would. Throughout the day, I mulled over Hector's words "Opportunity is everywhere." I wondered what they meant. I wondered if I would even recognize an opportunity if I saw one.

I reached the Sanchez farm at dusk. "Good evening . . ." I said, looking up at the huge man before me. "Are you Sanchez?"

"What do you want?"

"Hector Ortega told me to stop here," I said, unprepared for Sanchez's brusqueness. "He said you'd let me sleep in your barn tonight."

"Hector, eh?" The bearlike man smiled and clapped me on the shoulder. "Haven't seen him lately. Come in, boy, I'll bet you're hungry."

Sanchez's wife gave me something to eat. It wasn't great like at Hector's but I was glad to put food in my stomach.

After dinner, Sanchez showed me and Teresa the barn.

"This is it," I said to Teresa after he left. "Tomorrow, we'll be in the city." Involuntarily, I shivered. "I wonder what's going to happen. What if I can't find work? We may end up begging on the street. Or worse, dead, in a gutter. How am I going to take care of us? All day I looked for an opportunity, but didn't see one."

Teresa nudged me until I lay down. It was time to sleep. I drifted off with her muzzle massaging the back of my neck.

The next morning I awoke early. But now that the day had arrived, I lay on my mat, paralyzed with fear. The city awaited me, but I was reluctant to get going. By the time Sanchez came in, I had saddled Teresa.

"I see you're almost ready to go," he said.

I nodded my head, unable to speak.

"Where're you headed, kid?"

"To Mexico City," I said, then added to give myself courage, "to seek my fortune."

"With the donkey?" he said. "You must have a lot of money."

"Not really." I was too embarrassed to tell him the truth.

"Where are you going to keep her? It will cost plenty to house her in a stable."

My voice dropped. "Oh," I said. "I hadn't thought of that."

Sanchez walked around Teresa. "She's a fine animal," he noted. "I'd like to buy her."

"Buy her?" I said, feeling lost. She was all I had left in the world. "She's not for sale, Señor."

"Too bad," Sanchez said. "It could have been a good opportunity for both of us."

"Opportunity, Señor?" I said, my ears pricking up. "What do you mean?"

"Well," Sanchez explained, "it would have been a chance for you to make some money and for me to have a fine donkey."

I never expected taking advantage of an opportunity to be painful. I licked my lips. "How much can you pay?"

"Depends. Would you consider financing her?"

"I don't understand."

"Let's say you sell her to me for a thousand pesos. If you leave her, I'll give you some of the money now. For the privilege of using her and only paying you part of the money, I'll pay you interest."

"You mean I'll get back more than a thousand pesos?"

"Exactly," Sanchez said. "Sell me Teresa and I'll pay you one hundred pesos now and one hundred pesos every month for the next ten months—a total of eleven hundred pesos."

The money was tempting, but parting with Teresa . . . I stroked the back of her neck.

"You might find someone who can buy her outright," Sanchez said. "But with no money, I don't see how you can keep her."

"Will you let me come back and visit her?"

"Anytime you want."

"And if things work out for me in the city . . ."

"I'll let you buy her back."

It sounded crazy. Sell Teresa. I loved her. She was the only member of my family left. On the other hand, it made perfect sense. The city was an unknown. I didn't even know how I was going to manage. How could I take care of a donkey?

"Okay," I said. "It's a deal." We shook hands and he went up to the house to get what he called my first installment.

Left alone with Teresa, I started to shake. "I'm sorry, girl, I have to leave you behind. But he said I can visit whenever I want."

Teresa licked my face. I knew she understood.

"I'm going to miss you," I said, burying my face in her neck.

Thankfully, our good-bye was short. Sanchez soon returned with the money. "You'll need this, kid, the city's pretty expensive. Now how about some breakfast?"

"Not now," I said. Facing the city alone was enough to take my appetite away. "Thanks anyway."

Excited and scared, I started the last leg of my journey. Thoughts whirled through my head. I wondered what kind of job I'd find. Would I make enough to support myself? Would I ever be able to buy Teresa back?

I fingered the pesos in my pocket. They gave me a little comfort, but still I had no idea what awaited me in Mexico City.

Challenges

T HE JOURNEY INTO THE CITY TOOK LONGER THAN
I expected. The uphill road, the blowing dust, and my
heavy saddlebags slowed me down.

It was just after noon when I began glimpsing homes. I
was getting close. Although my heart quickened, I felt sad.
Saying good-bye to the familiar was not easy. And I missed
Teresa. She was my last connection with the old and I had
left her behind.

I stopped a man on the street and asked, "Can you tell me
how to get to the *zócalo*?"

"Which *zócalo*?" he asked. "Mexico City has many."

"Isn't there one in the center of town?" I said.

"Oh, you mean *the* Zócalo. The Plaza de la Constitución."

I nodded my head. I was afraid to say anything more for
fear of sounding stupid.

"New in town?" he smiled.

"Just got here."

"Why the Zócalo? Nothing there but government buildings."

"I thought that's where I'd start looking for work."

The man laughed outright.

"Am I wrong?" I said. "Where would you start?"

"If I had the answer, I'd have a job myself."

My heart sank and my disappointment must have shown
on my face. "It's as good a place as any," he said, patting my
shoulder. "Good luck, kid."

His directions led me down the cobblestone streets of Paseo
de la Reforma. It was the most beautiful street I'd ever seen,

with huge houses tucked back away from the tree-lined boulevard. I wondered what it would be like to live in one of those mansions. Then I laughed at myself. I didn't even have a job.

It was early afternoon when I arrived at the back of the Cathedral on the north side of the Zócalo. While walking around to the front, the twin bell towers struck two o'clock. They also struck fear into me. The day was getting on and I hadn't accomplished anything.

Soon, though, I forgot my worries. The Zócalo stretched before me. It was enormous and made me feel small and insignificant. But the bustle of activity gave me some hope. Surely, in a city this size, I could easily find a job.

When some of the excitement wore off, I realized I was hungry. I walked to the nearby open-air markets, where I bought a drink. Then I sat down under a tree and ate the tortilla and dried meat Sanchez had given me. I watched people buying things in the market and couldn't wait until I had enough money to do the same.

Then I had an idea. After eating, I went back to the stall where I had just purchased my beverage. "Excuse me, Señor," I said. "I just got into town and need work. Could you use some help?"

"Not now," he said. "Maybe later on in the season, after my crop comes in."

"I'll do anything, Señor. I'll meet you early in the morning, help you set up and come back in the evening to take down your displays."

"No thanks, son. I just don't need it right now."

That afternoon, I visited the leather goods shop, the flower stall, the bakery, the candy store, the basket weaver, the candlemaker, the fresh fruits and vegetables stalls, and the silver jeweler.

All of them gave me different answers that meant the same thing: NO.

Before the market closed, I bought a sandwich. Tired and discouraged, I went back to the Zócalo to eat. It had been a long day and I decided to spend the night right there and get an early start in the morning. I soon fell into a deep sleep.

When the clock in the Plaza struck twelve, I sort of woke up. But I snapped to attention when I realized the gendarmes were arresting vagrants.

I grabbed my belongings and ran as fast as I could into the Cathedral. I waited, my heart pounding. No one came.

Relieved, I ventured out and found a secluded spot between the Cathedral and the El Sagrario. Although it was quite isolated, I still spent most of the night in fear of being discovered.

The next morning I woke up hungry and bleary eyed. My shoulders ached, so I hid my saddlebags in a crevice. Then I headed back toward Paseo de la Reforma. The day before I had noticed stores that were likely candidates for employment. My first stop was Lopez's General Store.

When I found Lopez inside, I said with a smile. "Hi, I'm Juan Gomez. I'm looking for a job."

"You and a thousand others," he said, shaking his head.

That wasn't the answer I wanted to hear. "I'll do anything, Señor—sweep, stock shelves, deliver groceries. Just give me a chance."

"Sorry," he said. "I'd like to help, but my boys do all that."

"Any ideas where I might try?" I said, fingering the dwindling pesos in my pocket.

Lopez chewed on the side of his lip. "You might try the livery stable."

Lucky Lopez's boys, I thought. They not only got to work alongside their father, but they had built-in jobs.

Señor Johnson, an American, owned the livery stable, my next stop. He was a skinny man with a face that looked like it had gotten caught in a vice. And he was just as sour as he looked.

"What makes you farm people think life here is any better?" he barked.

I felt as though he had slapped me. "I had no choice, Señor."

"Well, it isn't my problem. If you ask me, Mexico City is too big already. You'll end up in the slums like all the rest."

"I hope not," I said, backing out the door. Maybe it was a good thing he didn't have a job. I wasn't sure I wanted to work for him.

Across the street from the livery stable was a hotel. I went in. "How much for a room?" I said to a fat, matronly looking desk clerk.

She eyed me over her newspaper. "Twenty-five pesos a night."

I gulped. I didn't have that kind of money. "Can I work in exchange for lodging? I'll clean rooms, carry bags, anything."

The lady came toward me. She walked around me just the way Sanchez did when he wanted to buy Teresa. "Ooh," she said, patting my seat. "My women customers would just love you."

For a moment I stood there glued to the floor, wondering what she had in mind. Then I took flight. I ran out the door and up the street as fast as I could.

She chased after me. "Come back, good-looking," she yelled. "Let's talk."

Several blocks later, I turned and saw she wasn't following me. I stopped to catch my breath right in front of a shoe and boot repair shop. Before I lost my nerve, I went in and spoke to the owner.

"Hi," I said with a smile. "I'm Juan Gomez and I'm looking for a job."

"Do you have any experience?" he said.

"Not directly, but I've watched my dad resole shoes."

The man let out a sigh. "I could really use some help," he said. "Unfortunately, I don't have the time to train you."

"Please, Señor," I said. "I can do chores. I can help with customers so you can do your repairs."

"I'm sorry," he said. "It's just not a good time."

Tears filled my eyes. "What am I going to do? I have to find a job."

"Well, I wouldn't normally suggest this, but if you're really desperate . . ."

"Oh, I am Señor, I really am."

"Why don't you try the factories? There's a steel mill about a mile north of here."

"Thank you, Señor," I said. "Thank you very much."

Following his directions, I practically ran to the factory. I arrived at the entrance just as the shifts were changing. Deciding to wait a few minutes, I sat down outside the gate. Lots of young people walked past me. They looked so tired. Finally, I asked one of them, "How long have you worked here?"

"About two months," he said.

"How many hours a day do you work?"

"Twelve to sixteen," he said, and kept on walking.

Twelve to sixteen, I thought. Can't be much worse than farming. I stood up to go into the employment office but encountered four sickly men being pushed out into the street by some muscle-bound thugs. The men looked deathly ill, their cheeks sunken, their eyes dazed as they staggered away.

The last brute stopped before going back in and said to me, "Looking for a job, kid? We have four openings."

Stunned and sick to my stomach, I turned and walked away.

It was getting dark when I reached city center. Another day gone and I hadn't found a job.

Starving, I stopped at a little café and bought the cheapest dinner for the most food. When I finished, I returned to my isolated cubbyhole and lay down. I tried not to dwell on my situation because if I did, I knew I wouldn't sleep.

Several hours later, I woke up with severe stomach cramps and vomited. So much for cheap dinners. I spent the rest of the night slipping in and out of consciousness.

The next morning, I didn't feel like getting up. What's the use? I'm never going to find a job. I could go to the factories and die or I could just die now and get it over with.

Soon, however, I roused myself. I still had a little money. All was not lost. Not yet anyway.

Leaving my saddlebags in the same hiding place, I started walking. Soon, I passed a bakery. Even though I disliked sweets, the smell enticed me in.

"I'm willing to work for food," I said to the woman who offered to seat me.

"You alone?" she said, touching my shoulder.

I nodded, but prepared to run just in case she was like the woman in the hotel.

"Maybe I can have you . . ."

Suddenly, the door to the back opened. A rotund man in a white apron appeared. "Delores," he said, putting his hands on his hips. "What're you doing?"

"We can hire him. No?"

"NO!" he bellowed. "We have too many already." Then he addressed me in the same tone, "Go apply at the factories, just get out of here."

My face felt hot. The customers were all staring. Another no, and this one in front of so many people. Mortified, I left. I sat down out front, pondering my next move.

Delores followed me. "He's in the back again. Here, take this." She handed me a *boñuelo*. Then she leaned closer. "The factories work you hard and pay little." She shook her head. "Too many die."

I shrugged. "I need a job."

"Try Pedro's," she whispered.

I turned to ask, "What's Pedro's?" but she had already disappeared inside.

It was hot. I was discouraged and thirsty. I bought a *chía refresco* and sat down to rest in the Plaza. I envied the people walking by. It seemed they all had someplace to go, some purpose, someone to belong to. I felt so lonely. So far, Mexico City had been as unrelenting as life under Señor Hernandez.

Walking down Paseo de la Reforma, I asked six or seven people if they'd heard of Pedro's. Finally, someone said, "It's a restaurant," and gave me directions.

A restaurant. Food. I stepped up my pace. From Paseo de la Reforma and Avenida del los Insurgentes, I headed south and soon entered a posh area and located Pedro's.

Stopping across the street, I stared at the green canopied entrance. This was where I wanted to be in life. I imagined myself as a regular customer. My daydream filled me with courage.

Just as I was about to walk in, I caught my reflection in the glass. I was covered with a yellowish dust. Knowing I couldn't apply at such an exclusive place looking like I did, I went all the way back for some clean clothes.

At the Cathedral, I got a change of clothes and went to a bathhouse. There, in exchange for a few *centavos,* a clerk handed me a towel, a brush, and some soap. Then she led me to a room with a zinc bathtub.

The water warmed and soothed my aching body. Lulled by the music coming from the central room, I let myself relax until the water cooled. Then I shaved, dressed, and walked back to Pedro's.

This time I didn't hesitate. I straightened my shoulders, marched in, and asked for Pedro.

Soon, a short, chubby man came to greet me. He looked like he belonged in a barber shop quartet. "I'm Pedro," he said, wiping his hand on his apron before offering it to me.

I liked him immediately. "Juan Gomez . . . I'm looking for a job," I announced.

"What can you do?"

"Farming, mostly. But I'm strong and used to long hours."

Pedro twirled the end of his handlebar mustache for what seemed like an eternity. Finally, he said, "Come with me." I followed him through the dining room, dumbfounded. Dark blue velvet draperies encased the tall windows, white linen covered the tables, and gilded mirrors and paintings adorned the walls.

In his office, Pedro motioned me to sit in a chair across from him. "I do need a busboy and dishwasher," he said, pushing the black ringlets off his round face. "Twelve-hour shifts, six days a week. The pay is twenty-five pesos a week plus two meals a day."

"When can I start?" I said, thinking it sounded a whole lot better than the factory.

"How about right now?"

"I would, Señor, but I need to find a place to stay. I've been sleeping on the streets."

Pedro stared at me, twisting the end of his mustache.

"What could I do? The hotels are too expensive and the *mesones* are typhus infested."

Finally, Pedro said, "I have a shed out back. It's old and run-down, but you're welcome to it until you find something better."

I left to get my saddlebags. It was cool outside, already dusk and only six-thirty. I made it there and back in record time. I had a job. I finally had a job.

The shed was riddled with holes and ready to fall apart. But I didn't care. I had a roof over my head. I threw my stuff down and went into the restaurant for training.

Two hours later, Pedro came up to me and smiled, his eyes turning to slits under the mass of his high cheekbones. "You'll do just fine," he said. "Report tomorrow at six."

"A.M.?" I said.

Pedro nodded. "Think you can make it?"

"If not," I chuckled, "you know where to find me." Exhausted, I stumbled to my new home. At least there were no memories here, no gendarmes. Nothing to keep me from falling asleep, which I did immediately.

Several hours later, however, laughter woke me up. I peeked out one of the holes. The night shift was exchanging greetings with the morning crew.

I pulled out my extra blanket and lay back down. But I couldn't fall asleep. I started thinking about Teresa. Was she happy in her new home?

Finally I drifted off. It seemed like only a minute later, I was awakened again—this time by the sweet smell of pastries, an aroma soon joined by that of baking tortillas. The combination made my stomach churn.

I wanted to go back to sleep. But the grey morning light had settled in around me. It was time to get up. I dragged myself into the restaurant.

I worked from six to six. By midmorning, I had a snack, then, after my shift, I ate a huge dinner—followed by a noisy night in the shed. Except for an occasional evening walk, this became my routine. I was really quite lonely.

One day, Pedro asked me if I could cover for the evening busboy, who was going to be late. I eagerly agreed. Anything not to be alone for such a long stretch.

After my shift, I was eating dinner in the kitchen, when I noticed Juanita, the day cook, still there. "You're here awfully late," I said.

"I know," she said, glancing outside. "Pedro's wife is sick. He asked me to prepare their dinner."

"Are you upset?"

"I'm glad to do it," Juanita said. "But I'm worried about walking home alone in the dark."

"Where do you live?"

"On the other side of the Zócalo."

"What a coincidence," I said. "I live that way too. I'll be glad to walk you home."

Juanita looked relieved (and I was grateful that she didn't ask me exactly where I lived).

I watched Juanita move around the kitchen with ease. Although barely old enough to be my mother, she reminded me of a grandmother. She could have been attractive, but she dressed in baggy clothes and pulled her thick black hair back into a matronly bun. But her dark, lively, almond-shaped eyes convinced me someone special lived inside.

On the way to her home, we talked mostly about Pedro. "He's a great boss," she said. "If you're a good worker, he'll advance you."

"Advance?" I said.

"Sure. Waiters make more money. How old are you anyway?"

"Eighteen."

"Oh, I thought you were older. Here's my house." She turned toward me, her eyes sparkling in the moonlight. "Goodnight Juan," she said. "And thank you."

I felt good doing something nice for someone, but I didn't feel very good about lying to her. For some reason, I didn't want her to know I was alone.

After that, Juanita seemed friendlier. She always dished out huge portions for me if I ate before she went home. Otherwise, my life remained the same. I still went to sleep every night and woke up to the shift change and the baking odors. But I had neither the time nor the money to look for a quieter place.

One morning, after a particularly restless night, I sat down for a break in the kitchen and dozed off.

Juanita nudged me several times. "Wake up," she said. "You're young, you can take these long hours."

I tried to open my eyes but I couldn't. "Let me sleep," I said.

"You sick?" she said, her voice sounding concerned.

I stretched my back. "Sick of that shed." As soon as I realized what I'd said, my eyes popped open.

Her brows knitted. "You?" she said. "You're the one?"

"Juanita, I'm sorry. I didn't want you to know."

"Why not?"

"I don't know, I guess I was embarrassed. It was the shed or the streets."

Shaking her head, Juanita turned her back on me. I felt terrible. I'd ruined my first attempt at making a friend.

Occasionally, throughout the day, I saw her staring at me. But all I could do was hang my head.

Later, I ate lunch tucked away in the corner of the kitchen. Juanita approached me again. "Juan," she said. "I've been thinking . . ."

"Look Juanita. I'm sorry I lied. I'm only seventeen, I have no family."

"I know," she said.

"You do?"

"Yes. Pedro told me."

I started to say something, but she stopped me. "That was a nice thing you did the other night." Her voice softened. "What I've been thinking, I mean if you want to . . . it isn't much . . . but I could make room."

Now it was my turn to be confused. "Are you offering me a place to stay?"

"It'd be crowded with my three boys . . ."

"Thank you, but I don't want to impose."

"You wouldn't. Actually you'd be doing me a favor."

I stared at her. I knew she was poor too. "How much?"

"I don't want anything. It's more for my boys."

"How about fifty a month?"

"That's too much."

"Then I'll stay in the shed."

"Okay, okay," she said. "Come this evening and be careful walking the streets."

After work, I traveled the two miles to Juanita's. Even though all the houses were adobe brick with thatched roofs, I easily located hers. After picking up the lantern left near the street, I knocked on the door.

José, Juanita's oldest son, answered. For a minute, I was dumbfounded. He could have easily passed for a younger, stockier version of me.

"Come in," he said. I guessed he was around thirteen or fourteen, only because his voice had not started to change.

José led me into a small, square room that served as the living room, dining room, kitchen. The floor was dried mud. Juanita and her sons sat around the stone hearth. On it were a *comal* for tortillas, and a clay pot filled with beans.

Juanita stood. "Hello, Juan," she said. "We're getting ready to eat. Won't you join us?"

I sat down between the two younger boys while Juanita spooned the beans into wooden bowls.

Examining my new surroundings, I noticed a *metate* and *mano* poised in a corner. "When do you have time to grind corn?"

"Usually, Sunday mornings. This is Carlos," she said, handing her middle son his bowl, "my crusader. And this one is Paco, my little imp."

Carlos didn't look up, but Paco smiled. His front teeth were missing.

"Do you go to school?" I asked José.

"For now. . . ." He glanced uneasily at his mother.

"He wants to quit and get a job," Juanita explained. "I want him to finish this year."

"We need the money," he said, squaring his jaw. "And now—another newcomer."

"Juan's paying rent," she said.

"So were the others," José said.

"If you stay a long time," Carlos said. "Maybe I'll get to go to the university."

"What do you want to study?"

"Engineering," he said. "There's a half million people in this city and the water isn't fit to drink."

Juanita laughed. "He eats the most and stays the skinniest. All his energy goes to his brain."

I smiled. Carlos looked the role with tousled brown hair, an aquiline nose, and alert blue eyes.

"Are you our new daddy?" six-year-old Paco asked.

"No, little one." I smiled and patted his head. His straight black hair circled his face like a halo and felt silky beneath my fingertips. With black eyes, a small turned-up nose, and translucent skin, he reminded me of a China doll.

"I like you," Paco said. "I hope you stay forever."

"Okay, boys," Juanita said. "Time for bed, school tomorrow."

I glanced over at José. He was glaring at me. Unconsciously, I felt my jaw. Mine was squarer, my face thinner, but other than that . . . maybe that's why Juanita offered to take me in.

José picked up his mat, took the extra lantern, and led the boys into the bedroom.

Lifting the clay water jug, Juanita rinsed the dishes. Then she went to say goodnight to the boys.

Left alone, I circled the small room. In the corner, adjacent to the kitchen space, was a small wooden table, the only piece of furniture in the house. An oil painting of Our Lady of Guadalupe hung above the table and on it were statuettes of Jesus, Mary, and Joseph, along with candles, incense burners, and two vases of fresh-cut flowers. This area brought the only color to the otherwise drab room.

"We don't use it much anymore," Juanita said, from behind me.

I stood still, unable to speak, the emotion in her voice was overwhelming.

"José Sr. was the religious one. He kept the family together spiritually."

"What happened?"

"He was killed ten months ago."

"I'm sorry," I said. I knew what it was like to lose someone you love.

"José was very close to him, and now, because he's the oldest, he's in a hurry to become man of the house."

"There's plenty of time for that."

"That's partly why I wanted you here."

"What would you like me to do?"

"I'm hoping your presence will take the pressure off."

"I understand." I would have liked a few more years myself. "Losing a father isn't easy at any age," I said.

Juanita's two-room home was humble and crowded, but it was a place for me to belong. It was quieter and more comfortable than the shed. And before long, we adjusted to each other.

The following Sunday, I slept late. When I stumbled into the living room, Juanita and the boys were waiting for me. "We're going to Chapultepec Park. Want to come?" Paco said.

I yawned, and thought about going back to bed.

"Please, come," Paco said. "Please say you'll come."

How could I say no. I got up and got dressed.

Located in the heart of the city, Chapultepec was packed with picnickers. Like us, they came to enjoy the green grass, the gardens, the lakes, and the cooling shade of some very old trees.

We had a great time. We strolled around the park and explored the castle, which had served as Maximilian's palace during his brief reign.

I can't say what specifically happened that day, but the boys' attitude toward me changed. The next night, Paco and Carlos asked me to help them with their homework. Paco's questions were easy, but Carlos's were much more challenging.

As I settled into my new home, I began to wonder how Teresa was doing in hers. During that next week, the desire to see her grew stronger. So, on Sunday morning, I went to the livery stable and rented a horse. At first I felt guilty about spending the money. But then I realized—Sanchez's installment was due.

Finding a Path

THE TRIP TO SANCHEZ'S WENT MUCH FASTER ON horseback. But still I worried. Sanchez might not be home. What if he denies owing me money? What if he refuses to pay? By the time I knocked on his door, I had worked myself into a frenzy.

"My husband's out in the fields," the Señora said.

"Can I see Teresa?"

"The donkey's with him."

"Señora," I said, fingering the pesos in my pocket. "The Señor owes me . . ." I gulped. "Money."

"Settle that with him."

I thanked her and walked slowly to my horse, wondering what I should do. I could wait, I could return next week, or . . . I could visit Hector. He did say he wanted to know how I was doing.

Maybe he was just being polite. Why would such a rich man care about me? But he did say I reminded him of himself at my age. Before I could talk myself out of going, I jumped on my horse.

My confidence skidded when the multicolored mansion came into view. It was bigger and more beautiful than I remembered. Terrified of rejection, yet hoping for acceptance, I knocked on the door.

Miguel smiled. "Señor Ortega was wondering just today what happened to you. He's out on the back patio."

I jumped down the steps and ran around the house, smiling in relief.

Hector sprung to his feet when he saw me. "I'm having a late breakfast, won't you join me?"

"You're going to think I come here just to eat."

Hector threw back his head and laughed. "You're looking well, my friend, the city must be agreeing with you."

I sat down across from him. Miguel magically appeared with a plate of eggs and tortillas. I had only two helpings.

"The city's beautiful," I said between bites. "So many people, I love the markets. Sometimes I get to work early and go with Pedro to buy fruits and vegetables for the day's menu. It's so exciting."

"Who's Pedro?"

"My boss. At first, I hated the city. But I got a job as a busboy at Pedro's—Pierre's would be a better name, the menu's in French.

"Strange, huh? Mexican food given a foreign name. I think he likes me, he offered me his shed behind the restaurant. But Juanita, the cook, found out where I was living and she offered me her home . . ."

I stopped dead. Hector had leaned back in his chair, his warm blue eyes twinkling at me. "Sorry," I said, "I talk a lot, huh?"

"I'm enjoying it, please continue."

"There isn't much more to tell. Juanita has three sons. The oldest, José, treats me . . . okay, but Carlos and Paco like me a lot. Carlos is very smart—sometimes when he asks for help with his homework, I have trouble. It's good for me, though."

"You're welcome to browse through my library, if you like."

"You have a library?"

"I certainly do," he said, smiling. "Tell me, what did you do with your donkey?"

I paused. The question slowed me down. "I sold her . . . to Sanchez . . . for money."

"That must've been very difficult."

"I don't have the time to spend with her. It's so peaceful here, so different from the city," I said. My eyes rested on a red and blue macaw perched on a limb. "Hector, you said you were poor once. How did you become rich?"

"It takes hard work, young man, hard work and determination."

I chewed thoughtfully on my tortilla. "There must be more to it than that. My dad slaved all his life and he died a poor man."

"Son, there are many secrets to acquiring wealth."

"There are," I said, perking up. "Please tell them to me."

"They wouldn't do any good unless you understood how to apply them."

"Will you teach me?"

Hector leaned forward. "Believe it or not, you've already taken the first step."

My eyes grew large. "I have?"

"Yes. You've decided you want to be wealthy."

"Saying I want to be rich is easy. But how? I only make twenty-five pesos a week."

"It'll take time and effort to discover your path. If you have patience, investigate opportunities, and believe it'll happen, it will. Patience, persistence, and self-discipline, coupled with hard work and determination," Hector continued, nodding his head, "will bring success."

Suddenly a robin flew down and skillfully pulled a worm out of the ground. A robin never had to question; he knew exactly what to do. "How do I find what I'm best at? Being a busboy takes all my time."

"You already told me you go to market with Pedro. It's the perfect opportunity to ask him about the restaurant. Busboys can advance."

"What if he tells me it's none of my business?"

"I think you'll be surprised. He'll be so flattered, he'll take an interest in you. By talking to successful people and emulating them, you'll become like them."

"That seems sort of dishonest. What if I'm not really interested in his business?"

"Don't lose sight of your goal. It's like building anything solid, take it one step at a time. Maintain a positive attitude, and be realistic in what you expect to achieve in a certain amount of time."

I looked up at the sky. The day was getting on. "I need to go."

"Want to see the library first?" Hector led me through a tiled kitchen that was as big as Juanita's house. Copper pots and pans peppered the walls. We followed a long hallway for a few steps and then walked through an arched entryway.

The library was huge, yet had an intimate feel—a marble fireplace, overstuffed brown leather chairs, and floor-to-ceiling bookshelves. An oil portrait of a beautiful young woman reigned over the place. I was about to ask who she was when Hector started telling me how his books were arranged.

He seemed to have a book on every subject imaginable. "Carlos wants to map out a drainage system for Mexico City," I told him.

Hector slid his finger across a row of books. "This one describes how Paris was designed."

"If it weren't for me trying to keep up with Carlos . . ."

"You're interested in learning, that's what's important. Here, take this one for fun," he said, handing me another book.

Hector's words made me feel good. "Thanks," I said. "And not just for these books."

At the gate, we shook hands before I climbed on my horse and galloped off. I turned around once and waved because Hector was still standing by the fence, watching me. He seemed so lonely. I chuckled to myself. I never thought I'd feel sorry for a rich man.

Sanchez greeted me with a bear hug. "Sorry I wasn't here earlier," he said.

"I made good use of the time," I said, massaging my ribs.

"Teresa's in the barn. Want to say hello?"

While running up the path, I heard her familiar bray. I rushed into the barn and she immediately began licking my face. "You look great," I said. Tears filled my eyes. "Your new master must be good to you." I brushed her beautiful chestnut coat and somehow had the feeling we were saying good-bye. She belonged with Sanchez now and I belonged in the city.

Soon, I heard Sanchez pounding up the path and I quickly dried my eyes. "Here's your next installment," he said.

"Thanks," I said, grateful that I didn't have to ask for it.

Sanchez leaned his immense body against a wooden railing. "Where did you get Teresa?"

"At an auction, Señor."

"You seem to have an eye for donkeys."

"Thank you—my father taught me." The words surprised me. Maybe I'd learned more from my dad than I thought.

"Teresa is working out so well," Sanchez was saying. "If you can find me another just like her, I'll buy her under the same terms."

My heart skipped a beat. "I don't know if I can, Señor Sanchez, but I'll sure try."

Back in the city, I returned my horse to the livery stable. "Señor Johnson," I said. "Do you sell donkeys?"

"Of course," he said. "Why?"

I don't think that man ever smiled. "I'm looking for one. How much?"

"Seven hundred fifty pesos," he said.

Although they were too expensive for me, I asked to see them anyway. They were also small and underfed. I left, wondering where else I could look.

Juanita and the boys were eating dinner when I arrived home. "Get something to drink and join us," Juanita said.

Before I filled my calabash gourd with water, Paco ran up to me with his arms outstretched. I bent down and picked him up.

He circled his arms around my neck. "We missed you today, Juan. Will you go to the market with us next Sunday?"

"I will," I said, putting him down. "You're getting heavy."

Paco giggled. "Sit next to me, okay?"

I sat down by the *tlacuil*. "Where's José?" I said.

"At a friend's doing homework."

"That reminds me," I said, reaching for my bags. "Carlos, look what I brought you."

Carlos broke into a big grin.

"Take good care of it—it's borrowed."

"Thank you, thank you," he said. "Will you read it with me?"

We decided to start the next day. I bit into my tortilla, and looked around the room. What a difference from Hector's. Yet, I loved this place and the people in it. It was my home.

The next day, Pedro told me about an animal auction held every Saturday night in the northeastern part of the city. I planned to go that weekend but ended up working late. I did, however, get there in time to get a good feel for the routine.

On Sunday, all of us went to the market. I was in a really good mood. I still had the one hundred pesos from Sanchez plus my pay from the week before.

Wandering around the crowded stalls, I thought of my mom. During the winter months, when it was too dry to farm, she embroidered clothing for Hernandez to sell in Pachuca. She was an Otomí Indian, and had learned from the masters. Her work was very popular.

Hernandez provided the raw materials and she created the exquisite designs. For her many hours of labor, he paid her a few pesos. Occasionally, we would go to the zócalo to buy vegetables and fruit. There was such joy in Mom's face when she saw her handiwork on display.

Suddenly, I felt the urge to buy something for my new family. I bought each of the boys a serape, and Juanita a shawl. For myself, I purchased a sleek black leather jacket. It was a little expensive, but I told myself it was okay because I spent a lot of time walking in the cool evenings.

That night when José got into bed, he covered himself with his new serape. "Juan," he said, caressing the blanket. "Thanks, it's the first new one I've ever had."

"You don't like me much, do you?"

José paused. "It's not that—I'm just more cautious. You're not our first boarder."

"What was wrong with the others?"

"They sponged off us, as if we had anything extra. Ever since Dad died . . . well, that's why I wanted to quit school . . . I just didn't want another stranger in the house."

"I plan on doing my fair share. I want you to finish school."

That night, José drifted off to sleep with a smile on his face and I snuffed out the lantern with one on mine.

The following Saturday, I practically ran to the auction. This time I had a chance to look over the animals before going inside. The room was warm, so I took off my jacket. My fingers proudly caressed the soft, tanned hide. It was so luxurious and I had bought it new. It symbolized where I wanted to go in life.

I turned sideways to watch the bidders. What subtle gestures—a finger flicked on the nose, a slight lift of the head. I hoped I wouldn't have an itch anywhere the auctioneer could see or else I might end up with an animal I didn't want.

The donkeys I liked sold for 275 to 300 pesos apiece. Even if I bought no more gifts for my new family, it would be several months before I could save enough to buy one.

On the last Saturday of October, while I cleared off a table, Sanchez and his wife walked in. "Good morning, Señor," I said, approaching them. "I was coming to see you tomorrow."

"We thought as long as we're in town, we'd save you a trip." He opened his wallet and handed me my next installment.

After work, I ran to Juanita's to pick up my money. Then, as the sun set behind the mountains in ribbons of reds and purples, I arrived at the auction. Looking over the animals, I found three possibilities, but after checking their teeth, I narrowed my choices to two.

In the arena, the auction was already under way. Again, I studied the way people signaled the auctioneer. I started to sweat. I'd never done this before. My dad always said, a good auctioneer works his victims into a frenzy, making them spend more than they wanted. I had to keep my head—three hundred pesos was my limit.

When one of my choices came on the block, the auctioneer started the bidding at fifty pesos—a little low I thought.

"Seventy-five," one man said.

"Who'll give me one hundred, one hundred?" The auctioneer spoke so quickly, I hardly understood him. I raised my hand.

"One hundred, I have a hundred. Come on folks, this one's a beauty.

"One twenty-five, one fifty, one seventy-five, two hundred," the auctioneer said, pointing in rapid succession. He was smiling now.

"Two hundred, two hundred. I have two hundred. Anybody give two twenty-five?"

I nodded.

"Two fifty," another man said.

"Two seventy-five," I said. I'd almost reached my limit.

"Three hundred." The auctioneer pointed.

"Three hundred, anybody bid three twenty-five. How about you young man?" He looked right at me.

I chewed on my fingernail.

"Three hundred going once, going twice." He raised the gavel to close.

I don't know what came over me. I wanted that donkey and I was afraid I wasn't going to have another chance. "Three twenty-five," I said.

The auctioneer looked smug. He'd done his job. "Three twenty-five, going once, going twice."

I closed my eyes, hoping someone would bail me out. Down went the gavel. "Sold to the handsome young man with the black jacket."

A boy came down the aisle and placed a piece of paper into my shaking hand. I sat and waited for my other choice to be auctioned. It went for two hundred seventy-five pesos. I wanted to kick myself, but there was no way I could have known.

At the cashier's office, I paid my very last peso and went to pick up my donkey. Finally, I parked the animal inside the stone fence at home and went to bed.

The next morning at dawn, the braying donkey woke Juanita. Soon, the rest of us heard Juanita yelling and joined her outside. "I can't figure out what got this animal going," she said.

"Donkeys are very protective, did you see anything un-usual?" I said.

"I thought I saw someone running away."

José shook his head. "I've heard rumors about the newcom-ers stealing from this area. Imagine, the poor stealing from the poor."

Juanita shrugged. "You mean the poorer stealing from the poor. Oh well, boys, as long as you're up, get some water to mix with these droppings. Let's patch up the holes in the house."

I expected Juanita to be upset; instead, she surprised me by reacting so practically.

The boys and I set to work, while Juanita went to start tortillas for breakfast.

Later, I rode the donkey out to the Sanchez farm. Instead of taking the turnoff, I kept going.

"How are you, my friend?" Hector said. He looked like the first time I saw him—straw hat, dirty white pants with holes in the knees.

"You're busy," I said. "I'll come back another time."

"This can wait," Hector said, resting his body against the shovel.

"Something's happened," I said.

Hector furrowed his brow. "Good, I hope."

"It means some extra money for me."

"Wonderful," he said. "Come on in."

Inside, I smelled coffee brewing. It took me back. Sunday morning brew had always been a ritual at our house. I half-expected to find my parents waiting at the table.

I followed Hector into the breakfast nook. There, I collided with the warm sunshine. "Wow!" I said. "This is a great room."

The glassed-in alcove jutted out from the house like a giant bubble.

Hector smiled. "It's my favorite place. Sit here and look out."

Thunderheads were forming on the distant mountains. "I'm inside, yet it feels like I'm outside."

Miguel served the coffee.

"Okay," Hector said, eagerly. "Tell me."

"Remember the last time I was here, I had to go see Sanchez?"

Hector nodded. "To collect some money."

"He not only paid me, he asked me to find him another donkey."

"Excellent. What did you say?"

"I told him I'd try. So I started saving every peso and last night I went to the auction . . . and . . . I bought a donkey."

Hector stroked his chin. "That's nice," he said, thoughtfully.

"I'm hoping Sanchez will like him enough to buy him," I said. Under the scrutiny of Hector's powerful blue eyes, my pride crumbled. "I thought you'd be excited for me."

"What's your plan?" he said.

"Plan?" I said, feeling confused. "Sell the donkey to Sanchez."

"I mean after that."

I sipped some coffee. I had no idea. "Keep working at Pedro's—I guess."

"You're going to sell him the donkey and . . . that's it?"

I bit my lower lip. "What else should I do?"

"Juan, in many ways, life is no different than this room. It was designed to be a special place. In the same way, you must design your life."

"But . . . I don't know how."

"You told me you wanted to be wealthy. Now plan your life accordingly. Focus on your goal until you achieve it."

I watched a cow chewing its cud in the pasture. Why did every creature in nature know what to do, except me? "I don't know where to start."

"Set goals—both long- and short-term ones. Goals can change as you go along, but design them so they help you attain your primary objective."

"I'm hoping to sell that donkey for eleven hundred pesos. I bought it for three twenty-five. Isn't that a short-term goal?"

"What if Sanchez doesn't want the donkey?"

"He did as of yesterday."

"What if he doesn't like this particular one?"

How stupid? I lowered my eyes. "I hadn't thought of that," I said.

"When you risk your money, you must know exactly what you'll do if your plan falls through."

"So I'm not stuck with a donkey?"

"Exactly."

"He can't do that, I bought it for him."

Hector sipped his coffee. "Suppose Sanchez refuses the donkey. What will you do?"

Nervously, I stood up. I reached into my empty pocket. "Oh, why'd I get involved in this?"

"Sit down, Juan," Hector said. "He'll probably take the donkey. But asking 'what if' will help prepare you for any eventuality."

"I can't think what I'd do," I said, shaking my head.

"Why not ask why?"

I sat back down. "Isn't that kind of personal?"

"How else do you find out? What if he can't pay and is too embarrassed to tell you? What if he doesn't think the donkey's worth the money?"

"I see. Well, I could reduce my price or . . . I could sell the donkey to someone else."

Hector perked up. "Good, good," he said. "What about making this a business?"

"A business?"

"Sure. Ask Sanchez for referrals, ask if you can use his name when talking to others."

I met Hector's intense gaze and my insides shuddered. I'd never been brave around strangers. "I could try, I guess."

"Sanchez offered you a potential opportunity. By thinking creatively, you can expand it."

"But why do farmers need me? They can go to the auctions, too."

"Most people don't know places like the auction exist. Others may not have the time or the expertise to pick out a good animal. You're offering credit, good service, and an excellent product." Hector nodded his approval. "Why wouldn't they hire you?"

"I did check the livery stable first."

"And you would've paid full price."

"How'd you know?"

Hector smiled and patted my hand. "Continue to educate yourself—you'll discover ways to save money and to become more efficient."

"Dad loved the auctions; I just took the knowledge for granted and never realized how valuable it was."

"And very profitable if you apply it to other areas of your life."

Storm clouds darkened the pasture. "I better go. I sure hope Sanchez buys."

Hector walked me out. "That's a fine-looking donkey," he said. "You've got a skill for picking them—cultivate it."

I thanked him and left. It was noon when I walked up the path to Sanchez's house. Be positive I told myself. "I brought you a donkey, Señor," I said when I saw him.

"You did? Let's have a look." Sanchez hurried toward the gate.

I lagged behind. Would he buy? Now I understood what Hector meant when he said: always have a plan and an alternate plan.

After going through his poking and prodding routine, Sanchez finally said, "Young man, you got yourself a deal. Teresa's out in the barn, want to see her?"

I nodded. Anything to get out of his sight so I could tremble alone.

In the barn, Teresa looked up but didn't recognize me. In a way, I was glad. She belonged here. "I understand, girl, my life's changed too," I said, stroking her neck.

Sanchez joined me shortly in the barn and paid me the one hundred pesos.

"Teresa seems real happy here," I said.

"She ought to, she gets enough attention."

"Señor." I gulped. "Do you know any other farmers who might need a donkey?"

"As a matter of fact—my brother saw Teresa last Sunday and asked me where I got her. You might talk to him."

I stopped to see Sanchez's brother on my way back to the city. He gave me an order and two referrals. My spirits soared. I saved the two for another time because black clouds darkened the sky and the smell of rain was riding on the crests of the wind.

Big drops pelted me about a mile from home. At first, my leather jacket offered some protection, but the downpour soon soaked me through to my skin. I vowed never to leave the city again without a horse.

Although the sun came out by the time I reached home, I was shivering. I walked in the door to a royal greeting. Juanita got me a towel, José pulled off my jacket, Paco got me a blanket, and Carlos got me some clean socks. "It's good to be home," I said, smiling.

"Are you staying in tonight?" Carlos said.

"It'll take me the rest of the evening to warm up." I huddled in my blanket and moved closer to the hearth.

"We thought we'd start reading that other book," Carlos said.

Later, we lit the lantern and started *Grimm's Fairy Tales*. Paco sat in my lap while each of us took turns reading. I closed my eyes, and gently rocked Paco while listening to José. His voice was changing. I loved being part of this family.

Developing a Plan

T HE FOLLOWING SUNDAY, I CALLED ON THE
referrals Sanchez's brother had given me. They told
me to come back in the spring, but they gave me
more names. I visited two and was again turned down. Tired
and discouraged, I went home. Oh well, I thought, I still had
my job at Pedro's.

It was a very busy time for me. Several times a week, I'd
meet Pedro early and go to market with him. My questions
were paying off. Whenever he needed someone to work
overtime, he asked me.

Although I was exhausted by week's end, I continued my
Sunday sales calls. Some days, I spoke to as many as six farmers. But after several months, I still had no new orders.

By mid–December, I had the money to buy Sanchez's
brother a donkey. But instead of feeling elated that I had
completed another sale, I felt depressed. I had no other business in the offing . . . no reason to save my money.

After delivering the donkey, I didn't feel like talking to
farmers. The overcast and gray sky added to my gloomy
mood. I didn't feel like going home either. So I went to see
Hector.

When he saw me, he put his gangly arm around my shoulder. "You look like you need a friend."

We sat down in the breakfast nook. A grayish-white mist
hung over the mountains, hiding their craggy peaks. "I
haven't made a sale since November."

"Just because the first two came easily doesn't mean the
others will."

"But I've called on some of them three and four times already."

"Excellent," Hector said, nodding. "People are beginning to recognize you."

"Hector, I feel like I'm wasting my time."

"Have patience, it's winter. If you're still around in the spring, they'll turn to you. Think of this as building customer relations."

"I'm pretty discouraged."

"Well, break for the holidays."

"Oh, that reminds me, I have something for you." I pulled an oblong box wrapped in red paper out of my jacket pocket.

"What is it?" With all the delight of a child, Hector ripped open the package. "Thank you, Juan."

"I know you're going to San Francisco, Merry Christmas. I hope you like it."

"Like it? No one's given me a gift in years," he said, fingering the pen. "Because I'm rich . . ." He cleared his throat. "Now about your donkey business."

"My what?"

"Don't give up—if nothing happens by spring—well, it's your decision."

I left Hector's still feeling out of sorts. The donkey business was going nowhere. How long could I continue without an order? I wasn't really happy at the restaurant, either. My job required no thought. But I wasn't trained to do anything else. I felt trapped.

My gloominess seeped over into the next morning, but I went to meet Pedro anyway. Going to market was a diversion I enjoyed. While waiting for him, Juanita and I discussed the day's specials.

Soon Pedro came in wearing a white small-brimmed straw hat trimmed with a blue band. He smiled when he saw me. "Ready to go?" he asked.

"Uh huh," I said. "Juanita and I have gone over the menu."

On the way, Pedro asked me questions about the specials. He noticed right away that I wasn't myself. "What's the matter with you today?"

"I don't know. I was just thinking about Juanita."

"What about her?" he said.

I glanced over at him. Obviously, he was using his hat to mat down his hair. But where it stuck out, it had dried into tight curls around his face. He looked so approachable. "She's so creative."

"How so?"

"It seems like she plans the menu loosely and then says if there's a good price on beans, then we'll do this."

Pedro smiled. "Juanita's an excellent chef. She has high standards and she keeps my costs down." He paused. "Are you interested in becoming a cook?"

"I don't know."

"Well, something's troubling you. What is it?"

I was quiet for a while, watching people bargain in the marketplace. "I'm bored," I said, finally. "I want to do something else."

Pedro stopped the cart. "I've been wondering when you were going to tell me that."

"You're not surprised?"

"I've been watching you, Juan. You're conscientious. And I'm pleased you're interested in how the business runs."

So Pedro had noticed. "Thank you," I said, proud and embarrassed at the same time.

"You know, Juan, someday, I'm going to need a good manager, maybe even a partner."

"What about your kids?" I said, surprised by this turn in the conversation.

"My girls aren't interested." He hesitated. "I'd like to groom someone like you."

My heart quickened. "Then, what's next for me? A waiter?"

"I'm not sure. Maybe the books . . ."

"Don't waiters make more?"

"Yes, but you're the quiet type. People like a waiter who's outgoing. At ease with the public."

I was shy, it was true, but I hadn't been around people much. "I can learn, Pedro. Please, give me a chance."

"Do you know the menu?"

I rattled off the names of the dishes in French.

Pedro picked up the reins and we began moving. He started thoughtfully twirling the end of his mustache. Finally, he said, "Do you know who Fidel is?"

I nodded my head, somewhat confused.

"I'll arrange for him to train you," Pedro said, standing up. "He's the best. People keep coming back because he offers good service." Pedro jumped down and unloaded a crate. "We'll give it a try. If it doesn't work, we'll find something else."

Later that afternoon, Fidel, a handsome man of about thirty, approached me. I had admired him from afar so I felt a little nervous in his presence. "Pedro asked me to start training you." He walked around me, twisting his mouth. "Our first order of business," he said, shaking his head, "is to do something about your appearance."

Self-consciously, I looked in a mirror. "What's wrong with the way I look?"

"For one thing—your hair. Go tell Pedro we'll be back in twenty minutes."

I'd never been around anyone like Fidel. He was so self-assured, so confident. People sensed it too, especially the women. Many of them turned their heads to have a second look while we were walking down the street.

After two blocks, we ducked into a barber shop. "Part his hair on the left, leave it a little longer on the sides," Fidel said to the barber.

When the barber finished, he handed me a mirror. My black hair fell in waves around my high cheekbones. "You are a master," I said. My face looked softer and my jaw less prominent. The haircut drew attention to my wide-set green eyes and away from my puggish nose.

Back at the restaurant, Fidel said, "Juan, you need to smile more, show those beautiful teeth. You're much too serious."

"I guess I have a lot on my mind."

"Who doesn't? While at work, put it aside. People will respond, you'll see."

I worked the rest of the day with Fidel and watched how he charmed his customers, and it wasn't only the women. He had a way with people. By quitting time, he had made twenty-five pesos in tips. "Let's go out for a drink," he said.

"I don't drink," I said, feeling shy about facing a new situation.

"It's time you learned. Besides, you have a date tonight."

"With who?" I said. I'd never been out with a woman. What would I say to her?

"Come on," Fidel said. "One drink, if you want to leave after that, I won't stop you."

He took me to Garibaldi Square. We ate in a crowded outdoor café. I watched people dressed in fancy clothes come in and out of bars and eateries. They stopped to listen to the mariachis playing on the streets.

The square was more than enough excitement for me, but not for Fidel. After dinner, he took me to a *pulqueria,* where only men are allowed. "I thought I had a date," I said.

"Not for another hour," Fidel said, and ordered us each a *pulque* with a tequila chaser.

That combination left me feeling lightheaded and nauseous. I'd reached my capacity. "I better go," I said.

Fidel protested, but I left anyway. It was already late. I wondered how I was going to get up the next morning. Once on my own, I started noticing different things. Garibaldi was located in a rough neighborhood. The men looked tougher. I could see gun outlines through their clothing.

Beyond the square, the streets were deserted. With no moon, it was dark and spooky. Suddenly, I heard footsteps behind me. My heart pounded. Was someone following me? Was it my imagination? I started running and didn't stop until I reached Juanita's. My system was on overload. I vomited.

The next morning, I awoke with a headache. My mouth tasted terrible and my eyes were sensitive to the light. I thought about not going to work, but I hadn't even made waiter yet. And not going to work meant no pay. I couldn't afford to do that.

Finally, I dressed and stumbled into the living room. "Juan, I waited and waited for you last night," Carlos said. "Where were you?"

I felt so disgusted with myself that I snapped at Carlos. "None of your business," I said. Then I left, feeling even worse for being so rude.

The crisp morning air soothed my pounding head. But I wondered how I was going to make it through the day.

The breakfast crowd was unusually heavy that morning. It took all my concentration and I don't believe I made a single mistake. I remembered to smile and stayed attentive to all my customers.

After the crowd dwindled, I sat down to a cup of coffee in the kitchen. I felt dizzy. Fidel came in while I was holding my head. He looked so refreshed. "How do you do it?" I said.

"You get used to it. Want to go again tonight?"

"I don't think my body could take it," I admitted, thinking neither could my pocketbook.

Shortly after, Pedro stuck his head in and said, "Juan, can I see you in my office?"

Juanita and I exchanged glances. I hoped my meeting wouldn't be too complicated.

"Come in, come in," Pedro said, gesturing to a chair.

I sat down and waited for him to speak.

"I'm real proud of you," he said. "Some of my regular customers have made good comments about you."

For the first time that morning, I really smiled. "Does that mean I get the job?"

Pedro nodded proudly. "I'm raising your pay ten pesos a week and you get to keep your tips."

"Thanks, Pedro," I said, standing up. "I won't let you down."

Even with the good news, I still had a pounding headache. I couldn't wait to go home and go to sleep. I needed a healthy routine to function properly.

That night, I apologized to Carlos.

But Juanita overheard me and interrupted. "I think we owe you an apology."

"For what?" I said. "I'm the one who took off and no one knew where I was."

"Maybe, but it's unfair of us to expect you home every night. You pay rent and you have the right to come and go as you please."

I smiled. "Next time I'm going to be late, I'll try to get word to you."

"We were worried about you, Juan," Paco said. "Don't you know you're like one of the family."

"Thank you, Paco." I hugged him. "That means a lot."

When Juanita and the boys sat down to eat, I went to bed.

During the succeeding weeks, I devoted myself entirely to the restaurant. I practiced what Fidel taught me: smile, make the customer feel important, and give good service. During this time I realized that the same principles applied to selling donkeys. The only difference: at Pedro's I had a captive audience, while with the donkey business I had to capture my audience.

Throughout the Christmas season, I honed my skills. But sadly, I realized that I was never going to get rich on a waiter's wages. So, on the second Sunday in January, I went calling on farmers again.

I didn't make a sale that first Sunday out, but I remained positive. On my way home, I thought about how much I had changed. I'd become more personable. With the ability to put my personal feelings aside, I concentrated more on the farmer and his needs. But most important, I started believing I could sell donkeys.

Life tested my patience and persistence to the hilt. Another three months passed before I finally met with success. My first encounter with Señor Gonzalez was typical of how my day went.

I smiled as if greeting an old friend. "Good morning, Señor."

Gonzalez looked up at me, shielding his eyes from the sun. "Where've you been . . . missed seeing you."

I jumped down from my horse. "Just making my rounds. How've you been?"

"Glad winter is over." He patted his stomach. "Ate too much."

"I know what you mean," I said, thinking that was never a problem at Juanita's. "Señor, spring is here. Have you thought any more about a donkey?"

"As a matter of fact . . . I told my wife the other day, if you came around again, I'd take a chance on you."

I almost jumped out of my skin. I'd asked that question a million times and had always received the same answer. "Thank you, Señor," I said, shaking his hand. "I'll get you one as soon as possible."

That day, I picked up six orders—four financed and two with a 50 percent deposit. I wanted to tell Hector, but it was almost dark, so I went home. After supper, we gathered around the hearth and read another fairy tale. I don't think I heard any of it. I kept trying to figure out how soon I could get those donkeys delivered.

My high spirits spilled over into the next day. Although Mondays were usually slow, I earned twenty pesos in tips. Pedro paid me and I had one thousand pesos in down payments.

I felt rich. After paying Juanita my rent, I went shopping. "It's Christmas in April," I said to my family when I brought in the gifts. I had purchased new clothes and shoes for all of us.

By auction time Saturday night, I had only seven hundred pesos—barely enough to cover the cost of two donkeys and renting a horse. After identifying four possibilities, I went into the crowded ring to wait.

The air inside was charged. It was spring and there was a greater demand for donkeys. Once the auction started, the bids shot through the air like racehorses leaving the gate at the firing of a gun.

When my first prospect came up for bid, a number of people entered the fray, and almost immediately, the price was one-fifty.

I raised my hand.

The auctioneer nodded. "I have one-seventy, who'll bid one-eighty?"

I felt dizzy; the pace was too fast for me.

At two-seventy, the auctioneer asked for two-ninety. I said, "Two-eighty."

"Two-ninety," someone else said.

I paused and let the auctioneer say, "Two-ninety, two-ninety, going once, going twice . . ."

"Three hundred," I said.

"Last chance, folks. Three hundred, three hundred, three-o-five, anyone. Going once, going twice . . . Sold to the young man in the black leather jacket."

I let out a deep sigh. Maybe I had these auctions figured out. I'd wait until the bidding slowed, then up the price a minimum amount. I tested my theory on the next one.

"Two twenty-five, two-fifty," the auctioneer pointed and said.

Silence. The auctioneer said, "Two-fifty, two-fifty, going once, going twice."

"Two sixty," I said, ready to walk away with a cheap donkey. But this time, I started another round of bidding.

"Two-seventy, two seventy-five," said the auctioneer, pointing. "Anybody give two-eighty? I have two-eighty, two-ninety, two-ninety."

I refused to let the excitement carry me away. Two seventy-five was my limit for that animal. It sold for three hundred pesos. Was I being watched? There seemed to be more bidding if I was interested in a donkey.

Throughout the next round, I remained silent and gave my nod at 325 pesos. I won the donkey. Since I had the animals I needed, I stuck around to watch the rest of the auction. My second purchase was the most expensive of the night. So much for my theories.

It was windy the next morning so I packed an extra canteen and some chinela root. I had hoped the wind would settle down, but it worsened. Visibility was almost nil. My horse stumbled in several potholes. That's all I needed, a horse with a broken leg. I'd have to pay Señor Johnson's exorbitant prices.

Finally, I let the donkeys lead. They are more surefooted and their eyesight is better. Then I just steered the horse in their footsteps.

Two hours later, wind-whipped and dusty, I arrived at my first stop. "You have a choice this morning, Señor," I said.

"Oh good. Bring them in the barn."

I led the donkeys out of the wind. The farmer looked them over and picked the most expensive one. These guys wouldn't go to an auction, but they knew quality. "A good choice, Señor."

"I'm really surprised to see you so soon," he said, handing me five hundred pesos. "I like your service, you should try the plantation twenty miles north."

"Plantation? I thought that was just a small settlement."

"Not any more. Some guy named Hernandez has been buying up farms—people are selling and moving to the city."

My blood boiled. Could it be the same man? If it was, he was stealing the land. "Thanks for the tip, Señor, I'll check it out."

Perhaps that's what was going on in the city. When I first arrived, Juanita lived in the poorest section of town. But lately I'd noticed barrios springing up to the north of us. Their conditions made us look like the middle class.

While riding, my thoughts turned to Hernandez. "Go to the city," he'd said. He'd wanted to get rid of me. Now, he's giving others the same advice—as if life in the city was any better. He probably lives in a hacienda and rides around in a carriage. Someday, someway, I'm going to get him. He's going to pay for what he's done.

By the time I reached my next stop, I was so eager for my status to surpass Hernandez's that I would have talked the farmer into buying the donkey even if he didn't want it. "Here's the donkey you ordered," I said, with a big grin. "She's one of the best, I bought her just for you."

"Gracias. Such specialized service." He looked the donkey over with an approving eye. "Wait here, I'll get your money."

After he paid me, I said, "I'll stop back in a few weeks to see how she's doing."

"Bueno. Bueno," he said, nodding.

I asked for referrals and he gave me three. I thanked him and went calling. At two of the places, no one was home, but the third gave me an order.

Suddenly, I felt deflated and didn't want to work anymore. I headed home. My head throbbed and I was dehydrated from the dry wind. I chewed on a hunk of chinela root, which quenched my thirst but did nothing for my headache. Hernandez was troubling me. I had to become rich and powerful. How else could I get even with him?

The fact that I had five orders and only a thousand pesos also weighed heavily on my mind. Even working overtime . . . I didn't see how I could do it. In one week, I'd collect my installments, but that wouldn't happen until after the auction. If I wanted to become known for fast, dependable, quality service, I'd have to manage my money better.

At the auction the following Saturday, I glanced around the far-from-crowded room. I hoped to get three donkeys. When my first choice came up for bid, the auctioneer said, "Isn't she a beauty, folks?" He paused for effect. "Tonight, we're starting the bidding at two hundred pesos. Who'll give me two twenty-five?"

I gulped. They never started a donkey that high, but I wanted her. I raised my hand.

"I have two twenty-five, do I hear two-fifty? I have two-fifty, two-fifty, do I hear two-seventy-five?"

I nodded.

"Three hundred, three hundred. Do I hear three hundred?"

A man in the middle of the room suddenly piped in, "Three twenty-five."

The bid was meant to shut everybody up and it did for a stunned moment. "Three-fifty," I countered. I wanted that donkey.

"Three seventy-five," he said. He was standing now, ready to do battle.

My heart pounded. I stood, too. "Four hundred," I said. Was everyone in the ring holding their breath along with me?

"Four hundred, going once, going twice." The auctioneer stared at my opponent. "Last chance, folks." Down went the gavel. "Gone," he said. "Sold to the gentleman in the black leather jacket."

Exhausted, I sat out the next two rounds and so did my opponent. When the next donkey came up for sale, I started bidding. I bid for two rounds and dropped out. So did he. At first I thought he was there just to bid against me, but then I dismissed that idea and decided he just knew donkeys.

When my next possibility came up, I held off. Finally, I raised my hand at three hundred.

The auctioneer said, "Three hundred, I've got three hundred, anybody give three and a quarter?"

My opponent came alive. Out of the corner of my eye, I saw him raise his index finger.

"Three twenty-five . . . ," the auctioneer said.

I nodded.

"Three-fifty . . . ," the auctioneer said.

My opponent raised his finger.

We were at three seventy-five. It was up to me. Only the donkeys I wanted were going for so much. The others went for two seventy-five to three hundred. My palms sweated. The auctioneer was about to bang down his gavel. "Four hundred," I said.

My opponent let it go. I won the donkey. Two donkeys for eight hundred pesos. My head spun. How could I afford to stay in business? I'd never have enough cash.

At the cashier's window, I turned and saw my opponent watching me. When I walked past him, he sneered. "Tough business, eh kid?"

"It sure is," I said, wondering if he even bought a donkey. Next time, I'd pay more attention. I shook my head; I didn't need another problem. I already worked twelve hours a day, attended auctions every Saturday, and delivered donkeys and drummed up new business on Sundays.

Suddenly, I felt bushed. The extra money was nice, but I was tired of worrying all the time. I considered filling my remaining orders and finding something else to do.

My attitude didn't improve after a good night's sleep, but I started my Sunday routine anyway. I delivered the donkeys, and halfheartedly visited several farmers. Why get more orders if it was going to cost a fortune to fill them?

Maybe Hector could help. Slowly, I made my way there. It was a beautiful day. The birds were singing and the sun warmed my face. Idly, I watched a vulture circle his prey and wondered if I had been someone's prey last night? Then I shrugged it off. The thought seemed ridiculous. Why would anyone bother about me, the son of a poor tenant farmer?

Hector's eyes danced when he saw me.

"Why do you work so hard when you can afford caretakers?" I said.

Hector pounded a nail into the fence. "I like the exercise." He had on that same straw hat. The hole was getting bigger. I couldn't understand why he dressed like a poor man. I would have given anything to dress like a rich one. Lowering my head, I kicked the dirt.

Hector watched me. "Miguel's famous *horchata* is ready. It'd be great with a couple of sandwiches."

I perked up. "I'm very thirsty. And hungry, too. Can you read my mind?"

Hector threw back his head and laughed. Then he put his arm around my shoulder and led me into the house. In the alcove, Hector ate a sandwich with me. "How are things going?" he said.

I sat staring at my drink, idly turning the glass in my hand. Finally I said, "I want to quit."

Hector raised an eyebrow. "Still no orders?"

"A few, but I'm tired of working all the time . . . and I don't have any money."

"Indeed." Hector crossed his arms on his chest. "That seems to be the plight of every working man."

"Well, it's all my fault. I spent too much on myself and my new family."

"Very generous," he said. "But as you learn how to make money, you must also learn how to handle it. You can't satisfy all your immediate needs and wants and not expect it to affect your future."

"I know, I learned that the hard way."

"Have you thought about a budget?"

I chewed on my lip. "I couldn't help going on a spending spree."

"A budget will help discipline you. You'll know how much is coming in and how much is going out. More important, it'll teach you to save."

"Save, I can't make ends meet now."

"I know it's difficult, but you should always pay yourself first and learn to live on the rest."

Miguel brought me another sandwich and I swallowed the first bite. "How can I stick to a budget when the cost of donkeys is too unpredictable?"

"If you learn to use money wisely, you can be generous and still prepare for unexpected expenses."

"I just feel like the problems are too overwhelming."

"Unless you overcome them, you'll never be rich."

"You said develop a business plan. I did that. I told the farmers to buy from me, pay when I deliver. I even promise a refund if they're unhappy."

"Sounds good so far."

"Sure, it's great for them," I said. "But I don't have any cash, and last night I could buy only two animals because they were so expensive."

"I see." Hector nodded. "That's what's really bothering you, isn't it?"

"It seemed to be only the ones I wanted."

"Maybe they were of higher quality."

"They were, but by a hundred pesos?"

Hector stared out the window. Finally, he said, "How many have you sold?"

"Ten," I said. "Three on installment, two paid in full, and five on order."

"That's excellent. You should be proud."

"I am, but it's going to take me so long to fill them."

"How about if I order a donkey," Hector said, a devious smile forming on his lips. "I'll pay you one thousand pesos now and take delivery in four months."

"That's not fair to you."

"Why not? I'm not in desperate need of a donkey. Besides, I think you deserve a reward for a job well done."

My visit with Hector renewed my energy, and the extra cash helped to purchase three donkeys. However, I still had problems. Someone else bid me up to 425 pesos a head.

Realizing that I needed a tighter control over my income and expenses, I bought a notebook to track my business transactions. Meanwhile, I kept up my hectic pace at the restaurant.

Learning about Trust

THE SUMMER FLEW BY. I AVERAGED A NEW ORDER every other week, and collected my installment payments twice a month.

Oddly enough, it was José who gave me an idea to explore. One August night, he pulled me aside. "I went looking for a job the other day in the silver mines near Pachuca."

"Oh yeah, any luck?"

"Not yet, but you know, they use a lot of donkeys to haul ore. Maybe you should try getting their business."

"That's a great idea," I said, wondering how it would be to see Pachuca again. "I'll check it out."

The next day, I went to see Pedro. "What do you think?" he said, pointing to his red and white striped jacket.

I didn't know what to say. "It's different," I said.

"It's my wife's idea. She says I look summery." He put on his white straw hat, which by now was his trademark and pointed to the new red sash around it. "I think I look like a barber shop sign."

"Turn around," I teased him. "Keep turning. Yeah, you do a little."

"Your days may be numbered, boy," Pedro laughed. He took off his hat and sat down, his eyes twinkling. "What can I do for you?"

"I've been thinking," I said, sitting down. "I'd like to take some time off."

Pedro folded his hands on the desk. "How much time?"

"Well . . . Mondays are pretty slow. Maybe a few of them."

Pedro looked relieved. "I thought you were talking about weeks. But still, what am I going to do without you?"

"How about hiring Juanita's son José. I'd be happy to train him."

"If he's anything like Juanita . . . okay, I'll give him a try."

José worked with me intermittently for one week. He caught on so fast that Pedro offered him a part-time job.

Now that I had freed up an extra day, I felt pressured to become more productive. The following weekend, I traveled to Pachuca, a little town surrounded on three sides by mountains.

Walking around the zócalo, I thought about my parents. I could see my mother delighting in people buying her handiwork. All the memories made me feel lonely. Luckily, the long ride tired me out and I fell asleep quite easily that night.

Early the next morning, I went to meet the foreman at the silver mines. "I'll check with my boss," he said, staring with beady black eyes. "You're so much cheaper than Trujillo."

I nodded. I had no idea who Trujillo was, but I made a mental note to find out.

After giving the mine manager my sales pitch, I said, "How many do you want?"

"We're expanding," he said, rubbing his finger over his lips. "Let's do this—bring me one and if I like it, I'll order four more."

I explained my payment terms.

"I'll pay cash on delivery," he said.

I didn't argue; the potential for a large order was incentive enough.

On Saturday, I left work and ran to the auction, hoping to fill three orders plus the one for Hector. I found many possibilities, but I wanted Hector's to be extra special. Approaching one of the keepers, I asked if he knew of any others for sale.

"A stranger just brought in six donkeys. I only glanced at them, so I don't know if they meet your standards."

"You think they'll be auctioned tonight?"

"I'm not sure. They may have arrived too late to be tagged."

"Can you show me where they are?"

He led me to a holding corral where the owners left their animals while checking them in with the management. That's when I saw her—the first donkey I'd seen who could rival Teresa.

I looked her over. Her chestnut coat reminded me of my old friend. I wondered if she had ever done any labor. Her weight and teeth seemed to be in perfect condition. I guessed her age to be between four and six years.

While I stood there admiring her, the owner came up. "She's a beauty, isn't she?"

"Oh yes, Señor. She going on the block tonight?"

"Unfortunately, I'm too late for registration."

"I'd like to buy this one—I'll pay you a fair price."

"You can have her for twenty-five hundred pesos."

My eyes returned the man's steady gaze, which was hard to do—he made me uncomfortable. I should have walked away, but I wanted that donkey. "That donkey couldn't bring that much even on the open market," I said.

"You seem to know donkeys. Why don't you make me an offer?"

The man's statement seemed more like a dare than a business proposal. "Seven hundred," I said.

He stared at me for a long time, twirling his big cigar in his mouth. "Why do you want this particular animal?"

"It's for a very special client."

"The manager said they're always looking for donkeys because some kid hangs around buying them. Is that you?"

"I don't know. Maybe. But I can pay you the seven hundred."

He lit his cigar. "You're right, she is special. But since I can't fool you, I'll sacrifice her for a thousand pesos."

That was the amount I sold her for. Hector had been good to me, and if I made no money on the contract, that was okay. But when I opened my mouth to clinch the deal, I said, "Seven-fifty."

"Nine-fifty," he said.

"Eight-fifty, and that's my final offer."

"You just bought yourself a donkey," the man said, and wrote up a bill of sale.

I spent most of the evening waiting for the others to be auctioned. The prices had gone up again, and after spending so much on Hector's donkey, I could buy only one. When I finally collected my donkeys, I looked at Hector's and felt pleased with myself—a fine animal, a good price. And a profit of 150 pesos.

I leashed up the two donkeys, climbed on one of them, and started home. Two men on horseback began following me right after I passed through the Zócalo. The clopping hooves echoed on the cobblestone streets as the strangers rode up alongside me.

"Excuse me, son," one of them said. "Would you mind stopping for a minute?"

I looked over and saw the familiar *kepi* on one of them. "Is it important?" I'd heard rumors about the gendarmes—they protected the rich and picked on the poor. "I'm in a hurry."

"This man here tells me you're leading one of his donkeys out of town."

"Not possible. I just bought these donkeys at the auction."

I handed him the bills of sale, and he looked them over. "Well, these seem to be in order. But this gentleman claims that this donkey"— he pointed to Hector's —"was stolen two weeks ago. That the donkey belongs to his oldest son."

"What makes you think he's telling the truth?"

The gendarme got down off his horse. "He says if it is his donkey, there'll be a double cross branded inside the back left leg, right above the hoof. Do you mind if we have a look?"

"No." I got down from the donkey.

Carrying a lantern, the gendarme walked around the donkey and lifted the left hind leg. There it was—the identifying cross. "You'll have to return this donkey to its rightful owner."

"But I just paid eight hundred fifty pesos for it."

The gendarme took the leash and let the owner lead the donkey away. Then he turned to me. "Let's go back to the auction and see if the man who sold you the donkey is still there."

We rode back, but the auction had shut down for the night.

"Now what?" I said, turning to the gendarme.

"I'm afraid you'll have to go to jail until I can verify your story."

"Jail! I just got taken for eight hundred fifty pesos. Why do I have to go to jail?"

"You're the one leading a stolen donkey, Señor."

Fighting back rage and fear, I managed to say, "But what about my other donkey?"

"We'll hold her at the precinct."

While walking into the police building, I looked at the gendarme. He was about my size and height, maybe a little older. He took me to his superior, who was seated behind the desk.

"Name?"

"Juan Gomez."

"Charge?" The superior never looked at me.

"Donkey theft," said the gendarme.

"Occupation?"

"Waiter," I said.

"Do you have any money or other valuables on you?"

"Three hundred pesos and a donkey outside."

Without looking up from his papers, the man behind the desk held out his hand. "Give me the money, I'll hold it here for you—as a deposit." He nodded slightly to the gendarme. "You take care of the donkey."

The gendarme led me back to a dark, dank, crowded cell. He unlocked the door and shoved me in. "We'll sort this out in the morning."

I sat down on a mat. The stench turned my stomach. I'd heard about people getting lost in the system. How long could they keep me for something I didn't do? Hot tears rolled down my cheeks. It could be a long time. All my hard work had come to this.

Just as it started to get light, the gendarme returned. "Gomez," he whispered. "Come here."

I walked to the bars.

"I don't see much hope for you," he said. "You'll either be shot trying to escape or . . . you'll be sent to the penal colony."

My insides trembled at the sound of his deep, raspy voice. If he was trying to scare me, he was doing a good job.

"Because I like you," he said. "I'm offering you your freedom."

I wanted out, but I didn't trust this guy. "What do you want?"

"Your leather jacket."

Slowly, I took it off and draped it over my arm. It was staying with me until I saw the exit.

Keys jangled, the cell door opened. The gendarme escorted me to an open side door.

As I flew out, he grabbed the jacket and roared with laughter.

Shivering, I hid behind a tree and waited. No one came looking for me. I hopped on my donkey and rode home.

Perhaps I should have been grateful—only three hundred pesos and a jacket I loved in exchange for my freedom. But I was mad. I was out a lot for something I didn't do.

Juanita sat up when I walked in. "What's happened? I've been waiting for you."

"I can't talk now," I said, heading for my room. I changed my clothes, took my last thirty pesos off the shelf and left to go see Eloy Chavez, the auction manager.

"Do you remember a man coming in late last night trying to check in six donkeys?"

Eloy scratched his head.

"Tall and thin," I said. "Had a bushy mustache, and an unlit cigar between his teeth."

"Yeah, I remember him. I told him he was too late, he should come back tomorrow."

"Did you happen to get a name and an address?"

"Since we couldn't do business, I didn't bother. What's this all about?"

"I bought a donkey from him—it turned out to be stolen."

Eloy looked shocked. "I'm sorry, Juan. We've never had a problem like this before."

"I just wanted you to know, in case he comes around again."

"Thanks for the information." Eloy stood. "Hope this doesn't affect our business relationship."

I left and dragged my tired body to an outdoor café, where I drank coffee and tried to think of my next move. Giving Hector the donkey wouldn't bring in any extra cash and I needed some right away.

Just then, two gendarmes walked in. My heart froze. They were coming toward me. Too scared to move, I shaded my face and sat very still. They took the table next to mine. I started breathing again—they'd come in for coffee.

I left the coffee shop, rented a horse, and rode to Pachuca. The foreman at the silver mine saw me and came out.

"Thought I'd take a chance you'd be here today," I said. "I brought you a donkey."

He squinted his eyes at me. "I don't do business with thieves."

"Huh?" I said, my face growing hot. I didn't know what to say, the accusation took me totally by surprise. "This donkey isn't stolen," I said, finally. "I assure you . . ."

"Get off this property before I have you thrown off. And don't come back."

I stared at him. How could he possibly know? Why did I feel ashamed? Obviously, he wasn't in the mood to listen, so I left. After delivering the donkey to one of my other customers, I wanted to go home. But I had something to do.

It was late when I arrived at Hector's. When I saw his kind face, I started to cry. Hector led me into the library and I sat in one of the leather chairs.

Miguel served hot chocolate. Its warmth soothed my stuttering chest.

"It's late," Hector said. "Can you spend the night?"

"José's working my shift tomorrow." I tensed up again. "Maybe I should go back."

"What's wrong, Juan?"

"Yesterday was a disaster. I'm such a fool. And—as you can see—I didn't bring you a donkey. But I'll get you one—I promise."

"I'm not worried about the donkey," Hector said. "I'm more concerned about you."

"That's more than I deserve. I've let you down."

"Juan, I trust you . . . and I don't believe you'd take advantage of my trust."

"That's what got me into this mess—trusting someone I shouldn't have trusted." I told him the whole story—how exhilarated I'd felt making such a good deal on the donkey, only to lose her hours later to her rightful owner.

"I'm sorry you had to learn such a painful lesson. But then, I always want to protect the people I care about."

My eyes filled up again. Hector handed me his handkerchief and waited. Finally, he said, "The mistake wasn't so devastating, what's the most you've lost? Eight hundred fifty pesos?"

"And the donkey I wanted to present to you, my friend."

"But you haven't lost my friendship. And your mistake will teach you about good judgment."

"I should've listened to my instincts. That man made me uncomfortable."

"Probably. But don't become suspicious of everyone you meet. There are more honest people in the world than dishonest ones."

"The man struck me as shifty, untrustworthy. But he had such a beautiful donkey."

"You might give him the benefit of the doubt, you know. Maybe he didn't know it was stolen."

I laughed, but the words "benefit of the doubt" stung. No one had given me that. I was assumed guilty.

"Someone out there has taught you how not to trust," he said. "There are times when that's appropriate, but usually trust in others encourages their trustworthiness."

I lowered my head and spoke quietly. "There's more," I said.

"I'm listening."

Again the tears burned behind my eyes and this time I could not control them. "I spent the night in jail," I said, finally. "The gendarmes took my cash, my beautiful black leather jacket, then released me out a side door. Now I have to start all over again."

"Chances are no one will know."

"That's what I thought too, but the word's out." I told him about the silver mine. "I may lose my job. I've probably already lost my reputation."

"Maybe someone set you up."

"Me? I'm a nobody, a poor boy. Why would anyone bother with me?"

"Juan, try to understand. Your success is bound to cause jealousy. Be aware of it, but don't let hatred and resentment consume you."

"Hector, I'm scared. If the gendarmes are as crooked as the man with the cigar, I don't stand a chance."

"You've done nothing wrong."

"I know, but the gendarmes think I have, the owner of the mine thinks I have, and God knows who else by now." I raked my fingers through my hair. "I don't know what to do."

"Just keep on trusting others, you'll find they'll try to do more for you."

"I almost believe that," I said, with a snort.

"It's true—and when you realize it, you'll be rewarded with increasing opportunity, luck, and success."

"Or they'll end up with everything of mine and I'll end up in jail."

"Always hold good intentions in your heart, or mistrust, hate, resentment, and jealousy will bring you down—emotionally and financially."

Neither of us spoke for several minutes. The blazing fire crackled its warmth into the room, and I closed my eyes.

Soon, Hector nudged me. "Come," he said. He led me through the living room, up a broad staircase, and into a blue bedroom. He lit the lamp by the nightstand. "Sleep here tonight."

I'd never slept in a real bed. "Hector . . ."

"Shhhhh," he said. "We'll talk about it tomorrow."

I dropped down on the bed and fell into an exhausted sleep.

Sunlight streaming in my window woke me the following morning. I rolled over on my back and folded my hands behind my head. This was the life—a spacious room, a bed, white lace curtains, a patchwork quilt, and paintings on the wall. In these peaceful surroundings, Mexico City seemed far away. Trusting my fellow man seemed easy. Maybe the gendarmes and the man with the cigar weren't that bad after all.

As I lay there, I kept staring at the two doors across the room. Finally, curiosity got the best of me. Behind the first was an actual closet—at Juanita's I stored things on a shelf. The second door opened into a full bathroom. I rubbed my eyes—a tub, a sink, and a toilet.

After using my private bath, I walked down the staircase, studying the paintings on the wall. At the bottom, there was a long hallway. I peeked into the living room. Although I couldn't identify the Persian rugs and French Provincial furniture, I knew they looked expensive.

The living room led into an informal sitting room, which flowed into the formal dining room. Oil and watercolor paintings decorated the walls. Most were signed, but the names meant nothing to me.

Finally, I reached the kitchen, where Miguel had the table set in the alcove. I settled back with a cup of coffee. It was a crystal-clear day and the mountains cut their craggy peaks into a cloudless blue sky.

"Good morning," Hector said. "How'd you sleep?"

"Wonderful," I said, looking up at him. "But part of me doesn't feel right."

"Stop being so hard on yourself." Hector sat down.

"I delivered a donkey on my way here, it was rightfully yours."

"Why didn't you bring it then?"

"Truth is . . . I needed the money. I took advantage of our friendship—yet you treat me like royalty."

"I make it a point," Hector said, finishing his coffee. "Never to take advantage of someone else's misfortune."

"That reminds me . . . ," I said.

Hector stood. "Let's walk, I want to show you the grounds."

We strolled through a wooded area. "There's something that bothers me, Hector. How do I know I won't end up like you, rich but alone?"

"I turned my back on many social opportunities because I couldn't see how they fit into my ambitions. You, I hope, won't make the same mistake. Be dedicated, but don't let it consume you."

"Right now, all I do is work. I don't know anyone my own age."

"Rank the things you want most in life—for example, business, companionship, and so on. After you've satisfied your first priority, move on to your next."

"I hope you're right about being able to have what you want most. But I want so many things, I'm afraid I'll be dead in a few years from exhaustion trying to get them all."

Hector threw back his head and laughed. "My boy," he said, "you bring so much delight into my life."

I smiled. I felt a closeness I'd never felt with my father. We never had time to just walk and talk.

A few minutes later, Hector said, "You started to say something earlier. What was it?"

"Oh, yes. Not long ago, a man asked me to find him a donkey. He seemed desperate, so I put him at the top of my list. When I delivered the donkey, he paid the first installment. But the following month, he said he couldn't pay, yet he begged me not to take the donkey."

"What'd you do?"

"I let him keep it, although I could've resold it."

Hector nodded. "You did exactly right."

"I thought about him when you said not to take advantage of another man's hardship. But I wonder if he tricked me."

"Why worry about it? If distrust lives in your heart, others will sense it and not do business with you."

"Sometimes I feel resentful because I've lost my parents. It's especially hard when I see families working, playing, eating together . . ."

Hector patted my shoulder. "What about the family you're with now?"

"Juanita and the boys are terrific. But they lean on me for support and sometimes, with all my other responsibilities . . ."

"I see," Hector said. "I think you're doing a splendid job."

I swallowed hard. Hector's support meant a lot.

"Can you stay for breakfast?"

"If I'm ever going to get you that donkey, I better go collect my installments. Thanks for sharing your home."

The sky opened up and it started to pour when I reached the outskirts of the city. After returning the horse, I walked home. But it was dark and I occasionally splashed the black pools of brackish water. By the time I reached Juanita's, I stunk.

Juanita and the boys had a good laugh before they brought me some clean clothes. Inside, I was struck by the difference. Juanita's living room, dining room, and kitchen together were hardly as big as my bedroom at Hector's.

I entered our community bedroom and set my saddlebags down. Juanita followed me in. "I've been so worried. I heard what happened," she whispered.

Her words supplanted my contentment. "Oh no," I said. "Do the boys know?"

She shook her head. "No, but it's going to be pretty hard to keep it from José."

"I'll tell him tomorrow."

Putting on a cheery face, I joined the group around the hearth. Paco put his arms around my neck. "I missed you at the market yesterday, Juan. It's fun watching you bargain."

I set Paco in my lap. "I'll teach you, so you can do it yourself."

I turned to José. "How'd it go?"

"Great—I really like the restaurant."

Juanita smiled. "He's good at it too."

My peaceful feelings returned by bedtime. All things considered, my life was pretty good. I had a growing business, some sound personal relationships, and a little money in my pocket. What more could I ask for?

Thinking Creatively

MY CONTENTED FEELINGS ENDED THE MINUTE we opened for breakfast. Although Pedro's was an expensive eatery, it took on a different atmosphere in the mornings, when it served as a meetingplace for farmers and ranchers.

On this particular day, many of the faces looked familiar—I'd sold them donkeys. I grabbed my pad and walked up to the first table.

"You weren't here yesterday," said one old rancher. "I thought maybe you were still in jail."

My face flushed. I stood there trembling, my feet glued to the floor.

"Prompt service, indeed," said another from behind me. "You stole from my neighbor and sold to me."

I turned to respond. "That's not true . . . ask . . ."

"And at such a good price," another interrupted. "Better to stick with Trujillo. You may pay more, but you won't have to worry about someone coming to take your stolen donkey away."

Finally, my voice came. "I showed the gendarmes my bill of sale. I didn't steal that donkey." No one listened. I dreaded approaching a new table because all I heard was: "Cancel my order." "Don't bother to deliver me a stolen donkey." "I won't do business with a thief."

I ran myself ragged that morning and received ten cancellations and no tips.

Before setting up for lunch, I went into the kitchen and sat down. "What a morning," I said, rubbing my temples.

"Sorry, little one," Juanita said, pouring me a cup of coffee. "I hate to tell you this, Pedro's looking for you."

I shielded my face, trying to hold back the tears. In two short days, I'd gone from happiness to despair and back again. I walked to Pedro's office. "You going to fire me?" I said, from the doorway.

He stared at me. "Maybe you should take some time off."

"No . . . please . . . ," I said, walking in. "I'm embarrassed enough as it is. To run and hide, that's like saying I'm guilty."

"I thought just until this blows over, but you're right. What happened anyway?"

After telling him, I said, "That gendarme exchanged my freedom for my leather coat."

"I'm confused. "Who's spreading the story then?"

"I don't know." I hesitated. "Ever hear of a guy named Trujillo?"

"Trujillo's a pretty common name."

"He'd be in the donkey business."

"Could be Art Trujillo."

"You know him?"

Pedro leaned back in his chair. "Never met the man. He's prominent though—has his hand in many different areas. Why?"

"Several people have mentioned my donkeys are cheaper than his."

"I suppose it's possible . . . but a man with Trujillo's money . . ." Pedro shook his head.

"You're probably right," I said. Trujillo sounded too important to be worried about a poor boy like me.

"Look at it this way," Pedro said. "Maybe fate is telling you to quit."

"But . . . I really enjoy it."

"It worries me you being out at night."

"If the bandidos don't get me, then the gendarmes will."

Pedro slammed his hand on the desk. "It's not funny, Juan. I don't want to lose you."

"Sorry, Pedro. I just feel boxed in."

"You still have the restaurant. You could learn the books until things settle down."

"No. If I stay, I stay on the floor. I'm innocent. I'll deal with whatever happens."

"And the donkey business?"

"I can't quit now. I have orders to fill . . . but I'll think about it." Standing up, I said, "I better get out there."

"Juan, I arranged for Fidel to come in early. I want you to go pick up some stuff at the market, then go home."

"Thanks, Pedro," I said, taking the list. "I'll see you bright and early tomorrow."

That night, Juanita brought home her specialty—*guajolote* with molé sauce. "How'd your meeting go?" she said, handing me a full plate.

"I still have a job."

"Why so glum then? If it's money . . . I have a few hundred pesos."

"Thanks, Juanita." Her offer brought tears to my eyes. "It's not the money."

"What then?"

"Those men think I'm guilty." I paused. "Thanks for this, but I'm not hungry."

I went outside and paced up and down the street. I wondered if Pedro was right. Maybe it was time to quit selling donkeys. Still, in or out, I had to clear my name. I just didn't know how. Chilled by the night air, I went in and went to bed.

The next morning, I lost another ten orders. The ranchers seemed to be saying, let's get the waiter while he's down before he becomes more successful than us. Hector had warned me to be aware of jealousy, but I thought he meant my own, not other people's.

On Saturday, I walked to the auction site. Before looking over the animals, I stopped in to see the manager.

"How goes it, kid?" Eloy said, patting my shoulder. "Here to buy more donkeys?"

"I have only one order."

"How come? Business slow?"

"Remember that guy with the stolen donkey."

Eloy scratched his head. "Never did see him again."

"Well, word got out. The ranchers canceled. They think I've been selling stolen donkeys."

"Why, that's ridiculous."

I nodded sadly. "Looks like tonight will be my last purchase."

"I'm sorry, Juan. Is there anything I can do to help?"

I snorted. "You could tell the farmers I'm innocent."

"How? You want me to become the town crier?"

"Not exactly. But you could tell the newspaper," I said, half in jest.

Eloy smiled. "Maybe I'll do just that."

"They're probably not interested. This ugly rumor got started by word of mouth. I was never accused officially. Thanks anyway, Eloy," I said, and went to check the animals.

I had one order to fill—Hector's—and just enough money. Right away someone started bidding against me. Since I was ruined in the donkey business, my previous suspicion seemed all the more ridiculous. People knew I had an eye for donkeys so if I was interested it must be a good deal. Still, I managed to get a fine one for four hundred pesos.

The next day, I left the donkey with Miguel because Hector was away on business. It was a relief to have that debt paid. On my way back to town, I felt sad. I realized I'd come full circle. I'd made my first sale after meeting Hector and now he was my last delivery.

During the next week, I devoted myself totally to the restaurant. People still stared at me and whispered, but Pedro's silent support gave me courage.

I worked the following Sunday because Pedro was short a waiter. It was just about break time when Juanita waltzed in wearing a big smile.

"What are you doing here?" I said.

She gave me a big hug. "I'm so happy for you."

"What for?" I said.

"Haven't you seen this morning's paper?"

"Nope," I said, loading up my tray. "I'll be right back." A few minutes later, I returned.

"Read this," she said.

There on page nine was an interview with Eloy Chavez. He talked about my buying donkeys at the auction every Saturday night. Concerning the night in question, he verified my story.

I looked at Juanita. "Do you think I'll get my business back?"

"I wouldn't be surprised. It should shut some of those big mouths up."

After that, I walked a little taller at work, but no one re-ordered. So I immersed myself in the restaurant. Pedro started teaching me bookkeeping.

Even though I kept busy, I started feeling like something was missing in my life. When the feeling nagged at me continuously, I decided to do something about it. I went to the auction.

It felt like coming home. This was where I belonged. Each flurry of bidding made me more determined. It was time for a change. If I wanted wealth, I had to go after it. I had to quit playing it safe like Pedro wanted.

The following morning, I went to see him.

"What brings you here on a Sunday?" he said.

"Sorry, Pedro, I can't do this anymore," I blurted.

"The restaurant business isn't exciting enough?" he said, after we sat down in his office. "I can give you more to do."

"Pedro . . . it won't work. I need something for me."

"Are you quitting then?"

Quitting? The thought had never occurred to me. "I just want Sundays and Mondays off."

"It's a bad decision."

"Maybe—but I have to try."

The next several weekends, I visited my former customers. I thought it would be easier to explain my innocence one on one. It wasn't.

Although many of the farmers were sympathetic, none of them gave me an order. Some said they would wait until next year, some claimed they'd purchased elsewhere, and a few ordered me off their property.

At the time, I thought the experiment failed and I gave up. I'd done all I could, now it was up to them. I couldn't continue to waste my time.

The following weekend, I rented a horse and traveled south toward Cuernavaca. It was a beautiful fall day and the leaves were just beginning to turn a golden color. I passed through the foothills and began the ascent over Tres Cumbres. The fresh air from the forest filled my lungs.

At Three Peaks, I stopped to take in the panoramic view. My worries seemed far away. I felt upbeat. I was going to rebuild my business.

Just north of Cuernavaca, I turned east and headed down into a fertile valley that produced rice, sugarcane, and tropical fruit. I spent Sunday night in Cuautla. During those two days, I visited some thirty farms and picked up only one order.

One farmer told me, "I'm a dying breed. With the plantations, bigger is better and cheaper."

I thought about Hernandez and how wealthy he must be by now. Consolidation, however, could work to my advantage too—one stop with multiple orders. "Señor," I said. "I'd like to do business with you, but I require a one hundred peso deposit."

He hesitated.

"Some of my customers don't . . . but it'll put you at the top of my list."

I felt a little guilty taking his money because at the moment he was my only customer. But I needed the cash to help defray my extra costs. I was starting over in an area farther from the city.

For three months, I spent most Sundays and some Mondays developing a relationship with farmers around Cuernavaca. I received only one more order.

I reminded myself that it took six months to get started before, but deep down, I resented having to begin again. If it hadn't been for that one incident, I'd have a thriving business.

Sometimes, while riding in the countryside, I'd dwell on my misfortune until I could think of nothing else. This mood would carry over into the restaurant, where I'd lash out at some farmer who still found it necessary to ridicule me.

One Tuesday morning, after another frustrating no-sale weekend, a rancher yelled from across the room, "I hear you quit the donkey business—run out of places to steal from?"

My jaws clenched. In a flash, I was at his table. I reached over and pulled him up by the lapels. "I never stole that donkey," I screamed.

Suddenly, a firm hand gripped my forearm. "I don't think you want to do that, son." Pedro's eyes were calm and steady. "Go fill the coffee pot," he said.

While I marched out, I heard another man, Salas, who did his share of ridiculing me, holler, "Why do you keep that little thief on?"

"I think you like to show off more than you think he's guilty," Pedro said, unruffled.

"You've been sucked in by the Donkey Man's charm."

I disappeared through the double doors and eavesdropped.

"You mean Juan, don't you?" Pedro said.

"Never knew his name, we just call him the Donkey Man."

"Juan's been employed here for over a year and, if you took the time to know him as I do, you'd believe in his innocence too."

I had to smile. Salas was speechless. And the room full of ranchers was dead quiet.

Soon Pedro came barging through the swinging doors and almost knocked me over. "Thanks," I said.

"I meant every word of it. Now get out there, you have customers waiting."

After that day, the snickering stopped. Perhaps it was just the loudmouth who had given courage to Salas and the others to ridicule me. He didn't come around anymore and the rest of the men treated me with respect—at least to my face. The name Donkey Man stuck, however, although I don't know why. At the time, I was anything but the Donkey Man.

A few weeks later, Señor Salas came in by himself and sat down at one of my tables. I walked up to him with my pad in hand. "You're late this morning," I said, trying to ignore the lump in my throat. "Your friends have been in and gone."

"I know," he said. "Bring me my usual, will you Donkey Man?"

"We're probably out, but I'll check." Without his cohorts, he seemed different—almost shy. "You're in luck," I said, setting the coffee and pastry in front of him. "It was the last one."

"Can you talk?"

"I have a minute."

Salas glanced around uneasily, then leaned forward. "I want to order another donkey from you," he said.

"You do?" I couldn't hide my surprise. "Why?"

"That animal you sold me is the best."

"Ugly, I recall you said."

Salas laughed. "Get me another just like it. Here's my deposit." He laid out five hundred pesos.

"You'll have it Sunday," I said. Outwardly composed, I walked into the kitchen, but inwardly my heart raced. What did this mean? If I pleased him, would he tell the others? Maybe I'd get some of my business back.

While walking to the auction on Saturday night, I wondered if something was going to go wrong. Nothing did. No one bid against me and I easily won the donkeys for 375 and 350 pesos.

When I delivered the donkey, Salas said, "This one's ugly, too."

I laughed. "At least you know it's no one's prize pet."

"Something came up this week. Can I pay you another hundred and finance the rest?"

I had no reason to help him. "Sure," I said. "Pay me at the restaurant." Encouraged that Salas didn't recoil at my suggestion, I continued. "I'm curious, Señor. Why the change of heart?"

"Several things." He stroked his chin. "That interview in the paper. Pedro keeping you around."

"Yet you went along with the one who harassed me the most."

"I know—I'm sorry. I guess I was angry and took it out on you."

"Angry? About what?"

"It may be just a coincidence, but after you quit, the price of donkeys went sky-high. I needed one but couldn't afford it."

"So you decided to use me even if you thought me a thief?"

"No. Since you had the guts to face all that public humiliation—well, I thought maybe you deserved another chance."

"I'm grateful," I said. "As before, I'll guarantee this animal just like the other. If for any reason you're unhappy . . ."

"Integrity . . . ," he said, nodding his head. "That's the other reason. A dishonest person would have taken this opportunity to gouge me."

I left Salas feeling overjoyed. Maybe he'd tell the others. Pedro would probably never forgive himself if he knew his sticking up for me helped put me back in business. I smiled. Pedro looked out for me. I appreciated that.

My next stop was down near Cuernavaca. Señor Baca came out, fidgeting with his hands. "I had no way of contacting you," he said.

"What's the problem?"

"I can't take the donkey."

"Why not?" I said. I was disappointed that I had traveled so far for nothing.

Baca let out a deep sigh. "Because . . . I can't pay."

What was I going to do with a donkey I didn't need? "We can make different arrangements."

"No—I just can't take it, don't ask me any more questions."

Frustrated and tired, I headed home. It was a bright, sunny afternoon. After several hours, I stopped to stretch out under a tree and almost fell asleep.

Soon, a peddler named Manuel approached me on foot. "What a fine-looking animal, Señor," he said, patting the donkey's neck.

Opening one eye, I studied the unkept man. "Would you like to buy her?" I said, mostly in jest.

"I would, but I cannot afford to pay." Pointing to a blanket spread under a big tree, he said, "I have some fine handmade jewelry over there, maybe we could trade."

I almost told the man I wasn't interested when Hector's words "opportunity is everywhere" rang in my ears. I sat up. "It can't hurt to look," I said.

At Manuel's shady spot, I knelt down and scanned his wares. A bracelet caught my eye. I picked it up and examined it. It was a handsome piece of silver, inlaid with turquoise and pearl. I never cared much for jewelry, but once I tried it on, I couldn't part with it. "How much?" I said.

"This piece—I'd normally ask three hundred pesos."

"Señor," I said. "My donkey sells for one thousand pesos—cash."

"You don't see any others you like?"

I glanced down at the blanket. "Not really."

Manuel pursed his lips. "How about the bracelet and five hundred now and the rest in two weeks."

"How do I know you'll have the money?" Even if I never saw the peddler again, I'd still make a profit.

The old man's face broke into a sly smile. "This is Holy Week, Señor. My business is brisk."

It was my turn to smile, sure the old man was hallucinating. But it didn't matter, I'd be rid of the donkey. So I took his bracelet and five hundred pesos and returned to my horse, where I pulled out my canteen and some tortillas.

Sitting under the same tree, I watched Manuel approach people just as he did me. Perhaps I'd underestimated him. He made three sales by the time I moved on.

I wore that bracelet everywhere. Several days later, I was at the restaurant chatting with Juanita in the kitchen when Pedro walked in. "An American in the dining room wants to meet you."

Following Pedro to one of our best tables, I wondered what the stranger wanted. People who came to see me—or used to—ordered donkeys. Surely that wasn't what this man wanted.

Pedro introduced me to Señor Taylor, who wore a blue silk shirt, white pants, and a lot of jewelry.

Taylor remained seated. He was tall and thin with curly blond hair, blue eyes, and a scraggly beard. Almost immediately, his long, bony fingers grabbed my wrist. "Where did you get this bracelet?"

Visions of the gendarme telling me I had to return the donkey flashed before me. I jerked my hand away. "Señor," I said, "I bought this bracelet from a peddler."

"Easy, son," the Texan said in his Southern drawl. "I wasn't accusing you . . . the bracelet caught my eye."

"Sorry," I said, settling down a little. "I like it too—it's not for sale."

"You misunderstand . . . I might want to buy some. Can I have a look?"

"Some?" I said, slowly handing him the bracelet. "I don't remember seeing any others like it."

Taylor studied the piece. Finally he said, "Where can I find this peddler?"

"Señor," I said. "Do you live around here?"

"I come down here quite regularly. Why?"

I pulled out a chair and sat down. "Well, I was just thinking, this bracelet is really unique and the peddler quite difficult. Maybe I should deal with him for you."

"Are you serious?" the Texan said. "I can buy from anyone in this city and have been doing so for years. What do I need you for?"

"In the first place," I said. "Manuel doesn't live in the city. Second, this bracelet is quality, but you don't know that every piece he turns out will look like this."

The Texan sat back. "It's true," he conceded. "I have made deals in the past, then come down to take delivery and either found not enough product or it was sloppily done."

"If you hire me," I said. "I'll guarantee the quality and a timely delivery."

"And if I don't like the product?"

"Then you don't pay."

The Texan examined the bracelet for what seemed like an eternity. Then he looked up at me with a faint smile. "Can you get me a hundred in two weeks?"

"Sure," I said, wondering if I could even find the peddler myself. I did some quick figuring. Manuel had said it was worth three hundred. But from my experience with donkeys. . . . "It'll cost you six hundred apiece," I said.

The Texan bit his lip. "Four hundred," he said.

"Five hundred," I said. "And that's my final offer."

"It's a deal," he said, shaking my hand.

"Señor," I said. "I will need a deposit."

Taylor pulled his hand away. "What for?"

"The peddler is poor. He'll need help buying that much material."

"You drive a hard bargain, son."

Taylor pulled out a large roll of bills and peeled off five thousand pesos. I stared at him. He'd just handed me the equivalent of five donkeys. "I guess I better go talk to the peddler."

I ran to tell Pedro that I had to leave. "We're very busy today," he said. "I need you here."

My heart dropped. I wanted to go find that old peddler.

"Why so glum?" Juanita said when I delivered her an order.

"I have an opportunity to make some money, but Pedro won't let me leave."

Juanita said, "I'm expecting José soon."

When José walked in, I cornered him. "Can you work for me right now?"

"I'm on my way to the bathhouse."

"How soon can you be back?"

My face must have shown the anxiety I felt. "I'll hurry," he said.

I watched the clock. I felt so jumpy. What if I couldn't find Manuel? I didn't want to lose the opportunity to make a lot of money.

An hour later José walked in and I dashed out. After renting a horse, I headed south at breakneck speed. When I reached the stretch of road where I first met Manuel, I slowed down. The lane was deserted so I traveled back and forth.

Finally, I sat down under a tree to wait and fell asleep. Some time later, I was awakened by two men haggling. I rubbed my eyes. One of them was Manuel.

When the peddler closed his deal, I ran up to him. "Manuel! Manuel!" I said. "I have wonderful news, I want to order one hundred bracelets just like this one for delivery in two weeks!"

Manuel scrunched up his chubby face. Then he started to chuckle. "Impossible," he said flatly.

"But . . . I thought you'd be happy."

"I am only one man. At most, I could make maybe forty."

"Forty?" I said. "But I need a hundred. I'll pay three hundred apiece."

"I could make that many if I quit selling, but this is what I love."

"How about three-fifty each?"

"Very tempting, Señor." He shrugged. "For that I could make maybe five more, but that's it."

"Forty-five, then, but they must be of the highest quality." Disheartened, I paid the stubborn old man a deposit. Too bad I couldn't convince him to do more.

Later, at the restaurant, I stopped to tell Juanita about Manuel. "It made me sick, all that money slipping through my fingers."

"What's with him?" Juanita said, taking her eyes off mine.

I turned around. Pedro had taken off his apron and was bending down to wipe the flour off his shoes. "Pedro," I said. "What are you doing?"

"I'm so glad you're here," he said, letting out a deep breath.

"What's the matter?"

"I can't believe it." He thumped his hand over his heart. "He's here, in my restaurant, after all these years. I really wondered if he was still alive."

"Who are you talking about?"

"I gave him the best seat, be sure he gets the best service, and, whatever he orders, make it look extra special."

I glanced over at Juanita and shrugged. Not even the president of Mexico had made him this excited. "Pedro! Who's so important?"

"Only the richest man in Mexico," he said, strutting through the kitchen like a peacock displaying his feathers. "Hector Ortega, that's who."

"Hector Ortega? The richest man . . ."

"Don't make him wait. Go. Take care of him."

"Let me comb my hair first," I said, running to the bathroom. My stomach felt queasy. "It's only Hector," I said to my reflection. "You've been a guest in his home." Why did I have the impression that he was only a rich recluse, not a well-known individual?

Pedro knocked on the door. "Juan, Juan. Hurry it up."

I straightened my bow tie. "Coming," I said.

"Do you have a menu, a pad? Don't make any mistakes."

"Pedro, you're making me nervous." He shoved me through the swinging doors and into the dining room.

I saw Hector immediately. He wore a white linen suit with a red silk shirt. His hair was freshly trimmed and hung in waves over his ears. He had the aura of a powerful, aloof man. I felt timid until his eyes met mine and lit up.

Placing a menu before him, I gave him a big smile. "Good afternoon, Señor, can I get you something to drink?"

"It's good to see you, Juan."

I wanted to sit down and talk. "What brings you to town?"

"I came to see you." Hector blushed and stared at the menu. "It's been so long . . ."

A lump gathered in my throat. The noted recluse left his haven to find me? "Can I get you some hot tea?"

"Please," he said. "And how about one of those fresh pastries you used to smell during the night?"

"I'll see if we have any left," I laughed.

As soon as I strolled into the kitchen, Pedro pounced on me. "What does he want?" he said.

"Tea and pastry," I said. I didn't have the heart to tell Pedro the truth—that Hector had come to see me.

Pedro scanned the picked-over desserts, searching for the best-looking one. He settled on a piece of four-layer chocolate cake with raspberry filling. Then he placed the pastry on a plate with a doily.

Hector loved chocolate. "Good choice," I said.

When I served the dessert, Hector invited me to have dinner with him at his hotel.

At a quarter past eight, I stood outside El Presidente Hotel, a graystone that occupied a whole city block. A huge green canopy extended from the front door to the street. Slowly, I followed the red carpeting through the doors, over the parquet floor, past the leather furniture, and between the hanging crystal chandeliers.

By the time I reached the clerk behind the mahogany desk, my mouth hung open. The place was so elegant. "Juan Gomez," I said, staring at the watercolor behind him. "I'm here to see Hector Ortega."

The clerk checked his cards. "Ah, yes, he's expecting you." And he gave me directions.

Outside Hector's door, I took a deep breath and knocked.

"Come in," Hector said. "I'm so glad you could make it." He escorted me to a long brown leather sofa.

"Hector?" I said, looking around the spacious room. "Do I embarrass you?"

Hector threw back his head and laughed. "Of course not. Where did you get an idea like that?"

"Well . . ." Now I felt silly. "Dinner hidden away in your room?"

"Juan, please, sit down." Hector's face looked apologetic. "I didn't want to embarrass you," he said.

"How could you do that?" I said. "You're not poor."

"You saw Pedro's reaction this afternoon." Hector shook his head sadly. "Sometimes a man's reputation so exceeds the man—he can no longer hope to live up to it."

I was about to ask him why someone so rich would worry about other people's opinions, but room service came with our dinner. The smell of roast lamb and fresh rosemary filled the room and I forgot about everything except eating.

When the server left, Hector said, "I've been looking for you every Sunday."

I stared down at my plate and mumbled, "I've been busy."

"Too busy to stop and say hello?"

My eyes filled with tears. "I didn't want to burden you, you've given me so much . . ."

"On the contrary, Juan. You don't know how . . . I've enjoyed . . ." Hector closed his eyes.

"How's the donkey?" I said, after a long, emotional silence.

"You mean Jessica?" He brightened. "She and Jesse get along great."

I watched how Hector used his knife and fork and imitated his actions. "And your business trip?"

"Not as well as I'd hoped . . ." Hector looked down at the table. "But I came here to find out about you."

"After the stolen donkey fiasco, I lost twenty-five orders in three days. Lucky for me, Pedro believed me."

Hector dabbed his napkin at his mouth. "Are you still in business?"

"At first I went to visit all the people who canceled individually. Even though they read the interview with Chavez, they weren't willing to give me another chance."

"I read that article, I thought it cleared your name."

"Well, it didn't. People are more willing to believe the bad."

"So you've given up?"

"Not exactly, I started working south." I sliced a piece of meat. "This lamb is delicious."

Hector smiled. "I'm glad you like it. It's one of my favorites." He took a bite and savored it. "At least it's all behind you now."

"Sometimes I feel the gendarmes are still watching me . . . it makes me very nervous."

"Just be patient, the longer you're around, the more people will believe you're reputable."

"It's hard. I get mad when I think of all that lost business . . . and then Manuel made things even worse."

Hector stood and motioned me over to the sofa. "Who is Manuel?" he said, pouring us each a cup of coffee.

I told him about the bracelet, the Texan, and the stubborn old peddler. "It's a great opportunity, but Manuel won't cooperate."

"Well, first of all," Hector sipped his coffee, "never take anything for granted. You assumed the peddler knew and analyzed his situation accurately. You didn't know most of the world operates in a limiting way."

"What do you mean?" I said.

"Most people automatically limit themselves. If they took the time to think, they'd see their options are endless."

"I offered him more money."

"Money's not his problem, time is. The peddler thinks he's the only one who can make the bracelets."

Amazed at Hector's accurate analysis, I said, "He did say, 'I am only one man.' But what can I do?"

"Think creatively for him. Ask if he has friends or family who can help, then he can fill your order and still do his peddling."

"You make it sound so simple," I said, standing up.

"Must you go?"

"It's getting late. Maybe I can get José to work my shift tomorrow."

"I understand," he said.

"Your . . . coming to the city . . ." I swallowed hard.

Hector put his arm around me. For a moment, I thought I saw tears in his eyes.

"I'll see you soon, I promise," I said at the door. Once out of the hotel, I ran all the way home. Juanita was waiting for me.

"Where've you been?" she said. "I've been so worried."

"I had dinner at El Presidente," I said, catching my breath. I sat down on the mud floor next to her. "With Hector Ortega."

"You mean that rich guy from this afternoon?"

I nodded. "I've known him quite awhile. He's been helping me with business advice. Tonight I think he gave me the solution to the bracelet problem."

"José can work your shift," Juanita said eagerly. "He said he wished he had something to do tomorrow." She cocked her head. "Why didn't you tell Pedro?"

"Don't know. It just didn't feel right," I said, reeling from the day's activities. "Good night, Juanita. Hope I can sleep."

The next morning, I rented a horse. I was filled with hopes of finding Manuel. After a frantic ride, I found him in roughly the same spot doing a brisk business. When he had a moment, I said, "I think I've solved our problem."

"I didn't know we had one."

"Manuel, I need one hundred bracelets, you said you could make only forty-five."

"Oh that." Manuel scowled. "I don't think I have time to make that many."

I gasped. I wanted more, not less. "What are you saying?"

"I have not started your order. You saw how busy I was this morning. My business has been like this for weeks."

"Manuel, you made a deal."

"I know, I still have more than a week. I'll start working at night. But . . ." He shook his head. "I'm going to be very tired."

"That's what I came to talk to you about."

"You care that I'm tired?"

"I see an opportunity for us to make a lot of money. I hate to lose it."

"Why change? I like selling. Things are okay."

"What if I gave you a solution so you could do both."

Manuel raised his eyebrows. "I'm listening."

"How about getting family or friends to help make the bracelets?"

Manuel scratched his head thoughtfully. "But that would take even more of my time. I'd have to round up those lazy bums."

"You could still sell during the day. You just said you'd be making bracelets at night anyway. Why not spend some of that time training them?"

"That's easy to say, but I doubt they have any talent."

"You'll never know unless you try."

"It sounds like too much work. I, too, am lazy."

I laughed. "That's why this would work to your advantage."

Manuel squinted. "How so?"

"Well, once you get your people trained, they can be working while you're out selling and you can have your evenings free."

Manuel stared at me for a long time. Finally his mouth turned up a bit. "You are a wise young man," he said. "I have a large family. We will produce your one hundred bracelets."

Making Money Grow

W ITH THE BRACELET PRODUCTION OUT OF MY hands, I thought I could relax, but the week after Easter was even busier. The restaurant's volume reached record levels.

On Wednesday, four ranchers—cohorts of Salas—came in together and ordered coffee.

As I turned around after serving them, one of them said, "Hey, Donkey Man. Heard Salas ordered another donkey from you."

I stopped dead and returned to their table, wondering what they had in store for me. "That's right," I said.

"I'd like to order one, too, but I don't want any stolen donkey."

"You're welcome to come to the auction with me," I said, looking him straight in the eye. "That's where I buy all my donkeys."

"Have your terms changed?"

"No, one thousand pesos cash or eleven hundred financed."

"I'll have to take my chances then, you're the only guy I can afford."

At the time, I was more concerned with my reputation than with my competition. "No man has ever lost a peso doing business with me."

"That's good," he said, "because we would each like to buy one."

I glanced from one to the other and each nodded. "Four donkeys?" I said. "It may take a while to get them, unless you want to give me a deposit."

They each handed me three hundred pesos. "I'll try to have them on Sunday."

Later, when I saw Juanita, I did a little dance. "I just got four orders, I may be back in business."

"I'm happy for you," she said, squeezing my hand.

"I guess it did some good to stand up to them," I said, mostly to myself. But I was too happy to accurately analyze my situation.

At week's end, Pedro called me into his office. "I'm paying everyone a 20 percent bonus."

"Great," I said. "I could use the money."

Pedro squinted. "For someone who's worked eighty-four hours, you're mighty perky. You have a date tonight?"

Chuckling, I said, "Only if it's with a donkey."

"Why take her out if that's the way you feel?"

"Pedro. I'm going to the auction."

"Oh no." His face dropped. "Why?"

"They came in here—four orders." I snapped my fingers. "Just like that."

"I wish I could say I was happy . . . but truthfully, I'd hoped you'd gotten out."

"I did—only because everyone canceled."

"Son," he said, leaning forward. "I'm afraid for you."

Pedro's concern made me a little jumpy. "I'll be okay," I said. "What could happen?"

~

After making those four deliveries without an incident, I breathed a lot easier.

It started to rain during my last stop, so I decided, since I was close by, to visit Hector. He was in the sitting room, reading a book. "Come warm yourself by the fire," he said.

Miguel brought me a blanket and I wrapped myself up in it.

"I'm returning your books. Thanks, we really enjoyed them."

"You'll have to take some more."

My eyes darted around the room. "Tell me about art."

"What do you want to know?" Hector marked his place and closed his book.

"It seems to go with money—Pedro has it in the restaurant, it's everywhere in El Presidente, and you have it all over your home."

"Art can be a good investment . . ."

"How do you know what to buy?"

"I buy what I like."

"Why did you buy that one?" I pointed to a painting of a meadow brimming with colorful wildflowers.

"It reminds me of spring, makes me feel happy."

"Was it expensive?"

"Not at the time, the artist was unknown."

I stood up and examined several. "I like your taste."

Hector smiled. "Eventually, you'll discover what you like and don't like."

"It doesn't matter, I don't have the money."

"Speaking of money, how was your visit with the peddler?"

I laughed. "The old man put up a fuss, but he finally saw the wisdom in your suggestion."

"Good for you," Hector said. "You understood the situation enough to explain it to someone else."

"It's exciting, all that extra money," I said, jiggling the change in my pocket. "I think I'll save most of it. I like knowing it's there."

Hector watched the fire. Finally he said, "You know, Juan, there are three types of people in the world: people who spend money, people who hoard money, and people who make money grow. I think you're ready to learn how to make money grow."

"How do I do that?"

"By keeping your mind open—you'll discover a world of opportunities that can offer you even greater wealth."

"Okay, where do I begin?"

"Right here," Hector said, pointing to his temple. "Develop a healthy attitude toward money. Think of it as nothing more than a fertilizer that enriches your quality of life."

"How do I know what to invest in?"

"When an idea or opportunity presents itself to you—research it, analyze it, be creative toward it—then, if it is a reasonable risk, act on it."

"What if I make a mistake? I could lose it all."

"Everyone makes mistakes, but you can minimize your risk by diversifying."

I wanted to ask more, but Hector yawned. In the waning light, he looked very old. Suddenly I felt scared. I had looked at him many times, but through the awed eyes of a struggling young man. Now, as he sat back with his hands folded in his lap, I studied his wrinkled face and wondered about his age. I prayed it would be a long time before I would lose him.

At breakfast the next morning, the lines in Hector's face looked less pronounced. Maybe all he needed was a good night's rest. After eating, we took a walk. He pointed out different areas and described how he acquired them. "Next time you come," he said, "we'll take the horses out. I'd like to show you the western edge of my estate."

"Hector," I said. "I don't know why you took such an interest in me, but I'm glad you did."

"Me too." Hector put his arm around my shoulder. "I really look forward to your visits. Can you stay for supper?"

"I'm sorry, I promised Juanita I'd be home early."

"Let's go get you some books."

We walked into the room and Hector was saying something about Homer's classics.

"Who is she?" I said, staring at the portrait above the fireplace. "Did you know her?"

Hector stopped. "It was in Paris—many years ago."

"Paris?" I said. "How did you get here?"

Hector stared at the woman with the bewitching eyes and walked toward her as if in a trance. "My parents were Spanish servants who worked for a wealthy French family. Their boss, DuBois, recognized my artistic talent and helped me get a scholarship to the Sorbonne."

No wonder Hector didn't look Mexican. I joined him at the fireplace, studying the painting. The woman was colorfully dressed, with an orange ribbon threaded into her thick black braids. She had high cheekbones, a button nose, and beautiful, full lips. Her brows were gently arched, and her eyes black as night.

"You painted this?" I said.

"I did it from memory. It was to be a wedding gift."

"How did you meet her?"

"At a café. Carmen was visiting from Mexico for the summer."

"Did she know your position?"

Hector nodded. "We had no secrets from each other."

I knew Hector had never married. "What happened?" I said.

"Before she left, we made plans for me to come here to meet her family. But I got scared, thinking they wouldn't accept me because I had nothing to offer her."

Hector paused and sat down. "I postponed the trip and went to DuBois for help. With his advice, I built up and sold several businesses."

"That must have taken some time. Why didn't you send for her?"

"I wasn't rich enough. The sad thing is I was so obsessed with making money that I didn't notice how long it'd been since I heard from her."

I sat down on the edge of the other leather chair.

Hector inhaled deeply. "Anyway, five years later, I finally bought passage on a ship, intending to surprise her. When I got here, she was already married."

"You've kept this on your wall ever since? It seems odd—continually reminding yourself of something so painful."

"Well, that's not quite what happened. It stayed in storage for years." Hector rubbed his forehead. "When I realized my money was worth so much more here, I took it as an opportunity to diversify."

"Were you hoping to win her back?"

"No. She was married."

Seeing the pain on Hector's face, I said, "You don't have to tell me anymore."

"I saw her all the time at social functions. It was so excruciating. I had all this money, but not her. Finally, I moved and bought this property."

"But this house is new."

"I built it for her."

"Now I'm really confused."

"We were reunited six months after her husband's death. It didn't take long . . . we decided to marry . . ." His eyes brimmed with tears. "I was so happy."

Reaching over, I touched his clenched fist.

After a long silence, Hector's eyes met mine. "She died a few months before I met you."

So that's why Hector seemed so lonely—he was grieving. "I can stay tonight if you'd like," I said.

"To tell you the truth, Juan," Hector said, wiping his eyes. "I'd rather be alone."

Placing my hand on his shoulder, I said, "I'll see you in a few weeks." As I closed the door, I heard Hector crying behind me.

I left through the kitchen. "Miguel," I said, noticing the hot chocolate set laid out. "You heard . . . ?"

"I was bringing it in—I'm glad he finally talked."

All the way home, the grief in Hector's voice stayed with me. I ached for him. Sometimes the trade-offs in life just seemed too harsh.

"Juan, Juan, we've been waiting for you," Paco said, when I walked in the door. "You're late."

"Something came up," I said, glancing at the piñata.

Juanita and José stared at me.

"Oh no," I said, cupping my hand over my mouth. "Juanita, I forgot. Where is he?"

"In the other room," she said.

My head pounded as I sat down next to Carlos. His face was buried in his arms. I massaged my temples. "Carlos," I said, "I'm really sorry."

"You promised you'd be here."

"I know," I said. The anguish in his voice brought tears to my eyes. "Someone—a friend—really needed me. I stayed to help him."

"Was he injured?"

"Not physically, but his heart was aching just like yours is now."

"You could've told him you had a birthday party to attend."

"When you need to cry, can you wait?"

"It just happens," Carlos said, turning over on his back.

"Sometimes it's the same with adults. My friend was suffering, I couldn't leave him."

Carlos wiped his nose with the back of his hand. "I love my new shirt and pants, thank you."

"Did your mom tell you that you have a pair of shoes coming too?"

Carlos threw his arms around my neck. "I'm not mad, Juan," he said. "I just wanted you here so badly."

"I'm sorry too," I said. "Look, I brought us another book."

That night, we read two chapters. After everyone went to bed, I sat outside with the lantern, bleary-eyed and exhausted, updating my accounts.

The next day, I went to meet Manuel. I hadn't seen him since I'd proposed Hector's idea and I was worried. Maybe I had left too much to chance. Perhaps I had spoken too soon when I guaranteed that the bracelets would be of the same quality. What if he couldn't finish the order, so he just took my deposit and spent it on something else?

Our meeting spot was deserted. Hector said to trust, but he also said to use good judgment. I paced in front of the tree. Where do I draw the line? How do I know what's appropriate? I looked up and down the road. No Manuel. I glanced at my watch; he was late. I couldn't wait much longer or Pedro would be furious.

Within minutes, I heard horses pounding the hard ground off in the distance. Soon, Manuel came speeding toward me. I relaxed—a little.

Once in front of me, Manuel smiled as if he had all the time in the world. "It's good to see you again," he said, tossing the reins aside.

I wanted to yell out, do you have the bracelets? But I held back and greeted him in the same courteous manner, allowing him to set the pace of the meeting.

Manuel stepped around to the back of his covered wagon. "It's been a tough two weeks."

I wanted to leap on him. "What do you mean?" I said, pacing my words.

"The hours have been long. I have trained many yet still continued selling."

What's he getting at? Does he want a reward? I bit my lip and said nothing.

Manuel pulled two bundles out of the wagon.

My heart raced as he brought them toward me.

He gave me an impish grin. "I hope you will be pleased." He squatted down and slowly unwrapped the blankets.

Quickly, I surveyed the lot. "Where's the rest?"

"I'm sorry, Señor. While your suggestion was a good one, my relatives have never made jewelry before. We started over many times."

I knelt down. "They're beautiful. I'm tempted to trade mine for one of these."

"I am pleased, too." Manuel's face glowed. "I didn't know my family had such talent."

I paid Manuel what I owed him. "I suppose fifty is better than nothing."

Manuel shrugged. "There was no way to let you know."

He was right, but his nonchalant attitude was so confusing. I told him how to find me in the future. Then I remembered something Hector said: In trade or in barter, sometimes you'll get more and sometimes you'll give more. Suddenly, I wanted Manuel to know I appreciated his efforts—I forgave the balance due on the donkey.

"I'm meeting the buyer tomorrow. If he wants the rest, how long would it take?"

"A week."

"You interested?"

Manuel smiled. "I would, only . . ." He stopped to assess my eyes. "Employing and overseeing people, Señor, takes much of my time. I would need more money per bracelet."

I laughed to myself. This old guy really is shrewd. "How about 375 per bracelet?"

Taking off his tattered hat, Manuel scratched his head. "Four hundred would be even better."

This time, I laughed out loud. I liked the old peddler. "It's a deal," I said.

Manuel broke into a toothless grin. "I won't let you down, Señor."

I rode back to town at breakneck speed. The horse's gallop seemed to match the beat of my heart. All afternoon, I hustled around the restaurant as if moving faster would make time fly. I couldn't wait to meet the Texan. I hoped the craftsmanship would overshadow the fact that I had only fifty pieces.

When the Texan came in at two o'clock the next afternoon, the restaurant was quiet. I took his order to Juanita, and went to get the bracelets. Calmly, I placed the first bundle in front of him and unwrapped it.

The Texan whistled softly. "Very nice," he said.

I smiled and nodded. "My jeweler outdid himself."

"Show me the rest."

"I separated them twenty-five to a blanket," I said, unwrapping the second bundle.

"Twenty-five? I ordered a hundred."

"You did, Señor. But I had no way of letting you know." The Texan had to allow that was true—just as I had with Manuel.

After a pensive moment, he looked up from the bracelets and said, "I have commitments."

"Give us another week—his people are trained now and ready to go."

The Texan leaned forward in his chair, quietly examining the bracelets.

I held my breath. What if he didn't take them? I would have to pay him back the deposit.

Finally he said, "I'll order fifty a month. However, I must have prompt delivery," he said, writing out a schedule. Then he pulled out a money clip bulging with neatly folded bills.

I watched in awe. Would I ever be able to do that? He counted out twenty thousand pesos and handed me the money. I folded the bills in half and put them in my pocket. "It's a pleasure doing business with you," I said, smiling.

More than anything in the world, I wanted to jump up and down and skip around the restaurant. A profit of seventy-five hundred pesos just did not happen every day.

Seizing Opportunity

HAVING EXTRA MONEY WAS A UNIQUE PROBLEM for me. Because of my humble beginnings, I wanted to hoard it. But I knew I had to find an investment to make it grow.

The sale to the Texan was my turning point financially. It boosted my confidence in my ability to sell. After several months, when Manuel proved timely, I asked the Texan if he'd like to increase his order. He did. To one hundred bracelets a month.

As spring blossomed into summer, the donkey business went into a rapid growth cycle. I received orders again. And, of the twenty-five cancellations, twenty-one came back— and many brought referrals.

My reputation as the Donkey Man spread. While that made me happy, it also caused concern. More people bid against me at the auctions. I paid almost five hundred pesos for a donkey.

As my income grew, so did the surveillance. The gendarmes left the more affluent neighborhoods to follow me home. At the time, I didn't mind the protection. But it bothered me that they watched from the shadows. It never occurred to me that I was getting rich. I still thought of myself as the son of a poor tenant farmer.

One morning, a plantation owner who lived in the city came into Pedro's and ordered four donkeys for delivery that weekend.

I wanted to tell him that I had others ahead of him, but the prospect of getting in with the big guys was just too attractive. "How do you want to pay?" I asked.

"On delivery," he said, writing down directions to his ranch. It was near Cuernavaca. How convenient—I was due to visit Manuel.

On Saturday after work, I went to the auction and purchased the four animals. With the higher prices, I wondered if the donkey business was worth my time. Pedro had balked about giving me every Monday off, so now I was free only the first Monday of the month. I spent that day collecting my installments due. That's why I wanted the plantation business—no collections, less travel time, bigger orders.

That night, I fell into an exhausted sleep. I woke up the next morning feeling feverish. But I had donkeys to deliver, so I dragged myself out of bed. I rode one of the animals to the livery stable with a pounding headache. After renting a horse, I followed the now-familiar path over Tres Cumbres. I tried to stay alert, but the fever made me drowsy.

When I entered the rolling hills, something agitated the donkeys. After glancing around and seeing nothing, I decided it was probably a snake.

Shortly thereafter, a voice behind me said, "Those are fine-looking donkeys, Señor."

My head snapped around. "Thank you," I said. Where had they come from? Three men on horseback, carrying rifles, with *panuelos* covering their faces. "What do you want?" I said.

They surrounded me. "Get down," one of them ordered. Another took the reins of the donkeys, while the third shot his gun in the air. My horse ran away.

I watched them dismount. "What're you going to do?"

"Nothing much," said the one in front of me. His eyes crinkled like he was smiling under his handkerchief.

"Well, be on your way then," I said, with bravado. "You have the donkeys."

My ploy didn't work. One of them grabbed my arms from behind and kneed me in the kidneys. I doubled over in pain. The rifle butt rapped me across the head, while a swift kick punched me in the stomach. Before I knew it, I was writhing on the ground being pummelled from all sides.

I remember blood spurting from my nose and one more sharp blow to the chest before the free-for-all ended. "Thanks for the donkeys," he guffawed, giving me one last swift kick in the ribs. "We'll make good use of them."

I passed out. I don't know how long I lay there, but when I came to, the sun was well to the west. Dried clots of blood dotted my hands and clothes. Vultures circled overhead. Those bandits had left me to die in the underbrush.

Dragging my shivering body toward the road, I hoped to attract someone's attention. I almost reached the clearing when I lost consciousness again.

"I think he's coming around now."

I tried to focus on the blurry outline of a man. "Where am I?" I said.

"It's about time, boy." The voice boomed from across the room. "I was beginning to wonder if you . . ."

"Pedro?" I attempted to sit up. "Is that . . . oooh." I fell back again.

"Take it easy, son. You've been hurt pretty bad."

"Here, sip some warm broth." Juanita's hand propped up my head. "You're safe, you're in the restaurant, Juan."

I drifted back to sleep and didn't wake up again until the next morning. Pedro was there when I opened my eyes. "Feeling better?" he asked.

I sat up, holding my head. "How'd I get here?"

"You were damn lucky, boy. A woman in the stagecoach saw you and told the driver to stop."

"They brought me here?"

"The driver asked where you lived and you kept repeating Pedro's. Luckily, a passenger knew of this place."

"Thanks for taking care of me."

"It's that damn donkey business again, isn't it?" Pedro said, shaking his head. "You want more to do? I'll keep you busy."

"Pedro, we've been through this before." I placed my head between my knees and rubbed my neck. "Some bandidos tried to scare me."

"Well, they succeeded in scaring me. You could've been killed."

"I know," I said, meeting his gaze. "When can I go back to work?" I had four donkeys and a horse to replace.

"The doctor said whenever you're ready. But today, you rest. Tomorrow, you can do book work."

I tried to stand; Pedro rushed to assist me. In the bathroom, I looked at my reflection. My right eye was almost swollen shut. Huge black and blue marks peppered my legs, ribs, stomach, and arms. No wonder Pedro wanted to keep me away from the customers.

Maybe I should listen to him and get out.

Just then, Juanita knocked. I opened the door and saw her soft brown eyes glistening with tears. "I brought you more broth. The doctor said to keep your fluids up."

Raising my arm to put around her shoulder, I grimaced. "Thanks, Juanita."

She helped me to a chair. "You hungry?"

I looked up at her and smiled.

"I know, you're always hungry." She left to get me some breakfast. I crawled to my mat and fell asleep.

The next day, Guerrero came to see me. "I heard what happened."

"I could replace the animals this weekend. But since the doctor says no hard riding for a while, I wouldn't be able to deliver them."

"You get them and I'll arrange to have them picked up."

"How about early Sunday morning?"

I gave him directions to Juanita's. "Because my price includes delivery, I'll deduct one hundred pesos per head."

After Guerrero left, I went to the livery stable to settle up with Señor Johnson—fifteen hundred pesos for that horse—and another two thousand to replace the donkeys. Quite an expensive weekend.

I stopped for a quick checkup with the doctor, and then went to buy a gun. I never thought I'd need to defend myself against another man, but if there was a next time, I wanted to be ready. According to Pedro, I was lucky it hadn't happened before.

For weeks after that incident, I was terrified to travel. I used my condition as an excuse, and actually delivered some donkeys in front of Pedro's. Eventually, though, I had to go out—the first of the month was rapidly approaching.

When it did, I collected my accounts without any trouble and stopped to see Hector on the way back. I told him nothing of the beating. Instead, I cut my visit short so I could return to Juanita's before dark. Then, that Monday, I went south to visit Manuel.

During the next several months, I spent a lot of time traveling. I was averaging three new accounts a week. Although I looked over my shoulder constantly, I continued because I was more obsessed with accumulating money.

One Saturday morning, a stranger came into the restaurant shortly after we opened and sat drinking coffee for hours. Then he ordered lunch and dessert. By midafternoon, when I gathered the last of his dirty dishes, I said, "I don't mean to pry, Señor, but are you expecting someone?"

He shook his head. "They told me I'd find him here."

"Who?" I said. "I know most of the customers. Maybe I can help."

"I'm embarrassed . . . I don't know his name," the stranger said. "They just called him the Donkey Man."

Dumbfounded, I stepped back. "Why do you want him?"

"I've a business proposition for him."

"You do?" I started to smile. "Well, Señor, you have found him."

"You? But you're only a boy!"

"I'm not, I'm almost twenty," I said, standing taller.

"You have quite a reputation, young man."

"What do you mean?" I said, hoping he didn't want to talk about stolen donkeys.

"Everyone I talked to considers you the expert."

"When it comes to donkeys, I buy only the best."

"So I've heard," he said. "Can we talk?"

I went to get some lunch. While piling rice and beans on my plate, I wondered what he wanted. He didn't have the hands of a farmer but then a plantation owner probably wouldn't. I poured him a cup of coffee and returned to the dining room. "By the way," I said, "my name's Juan Gomez."

"Juan," he said, "my name's Buford. Buford Jones. My employer, the U.S. Cavalry, needs a lot of donkeys for a special project."

"How many?" I said, taking a bite of my tortilla.

"Two hundred now and probably fifty a month—for an indefinite period."

The tortilla stuck in my throat. "You want me to get them?"

"I'm told you're the best."

"I'd like to help, but I don't know where I can find that many. How soon do you need them?"

"Yesterday." He chuckled. "But my boss would be satisfied with fifty a week over the next month."

"I'll have to ask around. I'm not sure there is such a supply of quality animals."

"I know, that's why we're willing to pay two thousand pesos a head."

My eyes widened. "That's a very fair price, Señor."

"I know that too, son, but it's a tall order." Buford picked up his hat. "See what you can do. I'll be back Monday morning for your answer."

After he left, I got orders all mixed up and upset several customers. His offer could be my ticket out of poverty. But how was I going to find that many quality animals?

Pedro pulled me aside in the kitchen. "What's wrong with you? People are complaining."

After a very long afternoon, I went to the auction with a pounding headache. I purchased three donkeys, and could have purchased five tops. I needed two hundred. Where was I going to find them?

I arose with the sun the next morning and delivered my donkeys. Then I went to see Hector.

Miguel answered the door. Although normally he treated me like a guest, this time he practically pulled me into the house. "I'm so glad you're here," he said.

"What's wrong?"

"Señor Hector has pneumonia."

The blood drained from my face. "Pneumonia?" I said.

"He's not been well for weeks. Remember when you delivered the donkey and I told you he was away on business?" Miguel shifted his weight. "He really went to see a doctor."

My heart sank. Hector had said his trip had not gone that well. "Can I see him?"

Miguel led me upstairs. "Señor Hector," he said, knocking on the door. "You have a visitor."

I was terrified to see Hector seriously ill, but I took a deep breath and went in.

He broke into a big smile and closed his book.

I breathed a sigh of relief. "You look better than I expected."

"I'm on the mend."

"Why didn't you send for me?"

"There was no need. Pull up a chair."

"No need? Hector, if something like this happens again, I want to know about it right away."

"Yes, boss." Hector gave me a mock salute. "Now tell me, what brings you out here?"

"I came to see you."

Hector stifled a smile. "I know there's something on your mind."

"I'm not going to burden you with my problems."

"Please do," Hector said. "My brain needs the exercise."

I stood up. "This isn't fair."

"It's very fair," Hector said. "Now, out with it."

I stopped pacing and stared at Hector. "The U.S. Cavalry wants me to find two hundred donkeys for them."

"How exciting. You're going to do it, aren't you?"

"I think not. I don't know where to get that many and I don't have time to look."

"Juan, how much do you make in a month?"

I fell silent, my eyes downcast.

Hector waved his hand. "You don't have to tell me if it's too personal."

"I never stopped to figure it out. The donkeys bring in about ten thousand and the bracelets—about the same."

"Can you afford two hundred up front?"

"If I use most of my savings."

Hector grew thoughtful for a moment, then his eyes began to twinkle. "There's only one solution," he said. "You have to quit the restaurant."

"Quit! I can't do that."

"Why not?"

"Those people are my friends."

Hector shook his head slowly. You have to be totally committed to your goal or you'll never get rich."

I felt hurt. "How can you say I'm not committed? I'm always working."

"Juan, you must become your own boss. Look at you—you work twelve hours a day, six days a week. No wonder you don't have time to find donkeys."

"But my job is my security," I said, fingering the pesos in my pocket. "What if something goes wrong?"

"You'll never get rich working for someone else. The best you can possibly do is survive. You work hard for others, why not work as hard for yourself?"

"It's easier, I guess . . . I don't have to plan my day."

"That's just an excuse. Take responsibility for your life. Working for yourself, *you* determine how much you earn and what hours you work. There's no limit to what you can achieve if you have the courage to break away."

"It's kind of scary . . . what if I fail?"

"What if you do? You can always go back to waiting tables."

Hector's words struck a hard, shattering blow. If I didn't give up my job and the life I'd grown comfortable with, I'd never be rich. I could no longer do both. I had to make a decision.

Learning to Diversify

ON MONDAY MORNING, BUFORD WALKED IN AND I met him with a pounding heart.

"Well, Donkey Man?" he said.

My breath stuttered in. "I accept," I said with more confidence than I felt.

After working out the details, I admitted, "I'm still not sure I can find that many animals."

Buford wrote down his local address. "Keep me informed, we'll work something out."

When the American left, I sat staring out the window. I had to face Pedro. Maybe I should ask for time off, just in case. I needed lots of courage to break away; I was scared of such a big change.

I found Pedro pouring over his books. Those numbers always determined his mood. "Pedro," I said, tentatively. "Can I see you for a minute?"

"Sit," he said, without looking up.

I stared at his matted-down hair. My news would probably make those curls appear a lot faster this morning.

Pedro jotted down a few numbers, then snapped his ledger shut. "What's up?"

"Pedro, I'm here . . ." I braced myself. ". . . to quit my job."

"What?"

I jumped. "I'm leaving the restaurant. I've got a customer who needs hundreds of donkeys."

"Those damn donkeys again." Pedro slammed his hand on the desk. "I should've put a stop to it a long time ago."

"Did you try?" I said.

"Why do you think I kept giving you bonuses? I wanted you to see the beauty of this business."

"I do, Pedro. It's just that this opportunity . . ."

"Opportunity?" Pedro lunged forward, placing his hands on the desk. "For what? To go out there and roam the countryside with the bandidos?"

I gulped. I had only thought of the money. Suddenly I pictured myself traveling those mountains all alone. He was right. It could be very dangerous.

"Change your mind, son. It's safe here. How does a partnership sound?"

I fingered the paperwork in my pocket. Should I call it off? "Let me think it over, I'll let you know."

Pedro's words threw me into a quandary. After talking to Hector, I thought I had the answer. Now I wasn't so sure. Pensive, I walked into the kitchen.

"Smile, little one," Juanita said, tickling me.

"I don't feel like it."

"What's wrong?"

"I'm so confused," I said. "I feel like my head's going to explode."

Juanita guided me to a stool. "Can I help?"

I told her about the cavalry man and the order for donkeys.

"What a wonderful opportunity, Juan."

"Yeah, that's what I thought too—but Hector thinks I should quit the restaurant and Pedro thinks I'm a fool. He offered me a partnership."

Juanita gasped. "What about his daughters?"

"I don't know, but I hate disappointing him. He thinks I'm the son he never had."

"What're you going to do?"

"I told the cavalry man okay . . ." I bit my lip. "Now I'm not so sure."

For a long while, Juanita didn't speak. Finally, she said, "What do *you* want?"

"Excuse me?" I said. For a moment, I thought she was Hector.

"What do you want *most*?"

"Money," I said. "Lots of it."

"Are you going to make it here?"

"Well . . . I could make a reasonable living."

Juanita smiled. "You have your answer," she said. "It's a risk. Do you have the courage to take it?"

I smiled back and got up to leave.

"The boys and I will miss you."

I stopped dead and turned around. Juanita had tears in her eyes. Again, her practicality had taken precedence over her emotions. "I love you, Juanita," I said, embracing her.

"You take care of yourself," she said.

Reaching into my pocket, I gave her a month's rent and three hundred pesos for Christmas presents. Then I went to see Pedro. "Pedro," I said, swallowing hard. "How about José as my replacement?"

Pedro's shoulders fell. "So you've decided to go, after all."

I nodded. "Look Pedro, I appreciate all you've done. I'm not doing this to hurt you."

"You'll come crawling back," he said, his jaw set.

"Then I will have failed."

Pedro looked me in the eye. "I'm scared for you, Juan."

"I'm scared too, but how else will I find out?"

Pedro stepped tentatively toward me and I reached out to hug him. Again, tears came to my eyes. "Thanks for everything." I turned around in the doorway to see Pedro blowing his nose. I was going to miss this place.

At the livery stable, I bought the horse I'd been renting since the robbery. My insides shook. This was a big step for the son of a poor tenant farmer. Oh well, I can always go back and find a job—probably anywhere but Pedro's.

First I stopped at the auction site for a visit with Eloy Chavez, the manager. "That article in the paper must have convinced that man not to show his face around here again."

"Thanks again for what you did," I said, unable to meet his gaze. That whole stolen donkey thing still made me feel embarrassed. "But I'm here on another matter."

"I only told the truth." I think he sensed I was uncomfortable. "So . . . how can I help?"

"I was hoping you could tell me about other auctions."

"Aren't my donkeys good enough?"

"The U.S. Cavalry wants me to find two hundred over the next four weeks."

Eloy let out a long, low whistle. "That's a tall order. I wonder . . ." After a moment's silence, he grabbed a map from the table behind him. "If I were you, I'd concentrate here." He pointed to an area southeast of Mexico City.

"Why's that?"

"The railroad."

"I don't understand," I said.

"I'm assuming the donkeys are going to Texas. How're you getting them there?"

I hesitated. "The railroad isn't completed yet, is it?"

Eloy shook his head. "That's why you work your way east, see? Put 'em on a train to Veracruz, then ship 'em on from there." Eloy grinned. "And—there's one other benefit."

"What's that?"

"Trains are harder to rob. The bandidos always stopped that stagecoach. Sometimes the passengers arrived in town naked."

I laughed. "Thanks for your help."

Before I left, Eloy said, "I have a storage pen available if you need it."

While riding to Juanita's, I decided not to catch the next train to Veracruz. If I found donkeys, I'd just cart them with me.

At home, I spread my map out and planned my route. I packed a few things and headed for Buford's office. "I've done some checking and this looks like the way to go." I explained Eloy's strategy.

"That'll save a lot of time." He filled out the necessary paperwork and handed it to me.

On my way out of town, I took a detour by Pedro's. I stopped across the street and thought about how scared I was the first time I saw the place. Now I knew the routine by heart: the busboys were setting up for dinner, Juanita was putting the finishing touches on her sauces, and Pedro was sitting in his office, tallying up receipts.

A tear trickled down my cheek. I no longer belonged there. A new adventure awaited me. It had been hard to say good-bye. My coworkers had become my friends, especially Juanita and Pedro.

I wiped away my tears. If I was going to make it to Texcoco for an auction that night, I had to get moving.

The rugged twenty-seven-mile trip took longer than I estimated. I arrived just in time and purchased three donkeys. Only 197 to go, I thought dismally. With nowhere to keep the animals, I traveled to the outskirts of town and camped.

At bedtime, I lay on my back with my gun beside me. Stars filled the inky night sky. It was beautiful, yet I missed the physical and emotional comforts of home. I wondered if Hector's rise to wealth was this lonely.

My doubts lingered the following morning. I needed forty-seven donkeys immediately. I packed up and headed east. Leading three donkeys over the steep terrain slowed me down. There had to be a better way.

In the next town, I left the donkeys in front of a restaurant and went in for lunch. I asked one of the customers about the auction.

"It closed weeks ago, Señor."

Discouraged, I drank some coffee, then gathered my donkeys and trudged on to Calpulalpan. There, I ordered a sandwich and ate it while riding out to the auction. Later I won two donkeys for three hundred fifty pesos apiece.

Afterward, I headed south toward Apizaco with five donkeys. Shortly after dark, one of the animals started braying loudly. Donkeys are usually surefooted, so I was surprised to see that one of them had tripped into a crevice and broken his leg.

I pulled out my gun. I had no use for a crippled animal. The shot rang out through the still night. I kept going. I wanted to put distance between me and the dead donkey.

While laying in front of a fire that night, I felt myself slipping into the depths of despair. How could I fulfill that contract? It would be impossible to parade fifty donkeys through the mountains. Finally I fell asleep and dreamed about the donkey I had had to kill.

The warmth of the sun peeking over the mountaintop cheered me. I forgot about my despair until I looked at the map. I still had a hundred miles to Orizaba and then another eighty some to Veracruz. This just wasn't working. I could've done just as well at home and kept my job at the restaurant. Now, instead of working alongside my friends, I was alone, traveling from town to town.

I packed up and started again. In my solitude, I led the animals over ridge after mountain ridge. And I said the restaurant was too predictable. Maybe Pedro was right. Dragging donkeys over rocky terrain and worrying about my safety wasn't much fun either.

Riding by some plantations, I toyed with the idea of selling them the animals and going home. Pedro would never let me hear the end of it. Neither would Hector, but for different reasons.

After twenty long, grueling miles that day, I made camp. The cloud cover helped darken my spirits. I wished for rain. If I caught pneumonia, I'd be too sick to continue. Then I could back out and still save my honor.

But daybreak came and I was dry. I headed into Apizaco, where the donkeys and I boarded a train. I'd had enough—enough of creeping along the mountainous terrain, enough of small towns.

Around noon, we pulled into Orizaba, a lush, fertile valley. Even though mountains surrounded it, the 4,100-foot elevation made it a refreshing change from the high terrain I'd been crossing.

But still I was depressed. The train to Mexico City departed each morning. Maybe I'd be on the next one. After renting a pen to store the animals, I relaxed in a long, hot bath and took a much-needed nap.

I purchased three animals that evening and didn't feel any better. I hoped a good night's sleep would improve my disposition.

It didn't. It was Thursday already and I had only seven animals—woefully short of the fifty I needed. A part of me wanted to give up, but I continued making plans.

After consulting a map, I traveled to Cordoba for an auction on Friday night and returned to Orizaba the next day. By Saturday night, I had purchased another nine donkeys. I could use the sixteen to fill my outstanding orders and forget about the cavalry.

Although the idea had appeal, I set up Orizaba as my base and traveled to neighboring towns, returning on Wednesday and Saturday nights for the auction. I purchased another ten animals—still not much better than if I had stayed in Mexico City.

While drinking coffee the next morning, I sat staring out the window. It's no use. I had found only twenty-six donkeys in two weeks' time. I didn't know what to do—go on to Veracruz or take them back to the city.

For a long time, I sat there, paralyzed with indecision. Finally, I collected my donkeys and bought us passage home. I tried to console myself as the train chugged out of the city. At least, I'd spend the holidays with my family.

What made me think that I, the son of a poor tenant farmer, could take on such a big responsibility and succeed? It was better for me to accept my place and go crawling back to Pedro. At least I'd tried.

But the farther the train moved away from Orizaba, the more depressed I became. I couldn't accept failure so easily. While staring down the steep ravines, an idea started forming in my head. Suddenly I jumped up and pulled the emergency brake.

The conductor came through the car, "All right, who stopped the train?" he said.

"I did," I said, standing up. "I need to get my horse and go back to Orizaba."

"I should throw you off. Don't you know we're in the steepest part of the climb?"

I let out a deep sigh. "Sorry," I apologized. "This is important."

In Orizaba, I sent Eloy a telegram asking him to feed and house the donkeys in that pen he had offered until I returned.

The next morning, I awoke early and headed for the auction site. After searching awhile, I found the assistant manager talking to one of his stable boys.

"Excuse me, Señor," I said. "Can I ask you a question?"

"What is it?" he said.

I bit my lip. I hated feeling so shy. "Is there a donkey breeder around here?"

"Why do you want to know?"

"I'm looking for a job," I said.

The manager glared at me. "This is a small town, boy. I know you've been traveling around, buying donkeys. Why should I send someone business that's now mine?" Then he stalked away.

I lowered my head in shame. Why didn't I tell him the truth? Now I'd have to ask someone else. Even after all the selling I'd done, I hated approaching strangers.

"Señor, Señor, over here."

I looked around and spotted the stable boy motioning to me from behind the far corner of the barn. I snuck over to him.

"I couldn't help but overhear. Sometimes he is so stubborn. I'll give you the information you need—for a price."

"How much?" I said.

"One hundred pesos."

I pulled the money out of my pocket.

The boy grabbed it before I could think about whether it was too high a price to pay. "The man you want is Francisco Vazquez. He comes to town every Monday and has breakfast at Emilio's."

"What time?"

He shrugged as if it were unimportant. "Late morning," he said and disappeared.

It was already ten-thirty, so I rushed to the diner. When the waiter came for my order, I said, "Has Señor Vazquez come in yet?"

"Haven't seen him."

"I'd like to meet him, will you point him out to me?"

"I'll tell Señor Vazquez you wish to meet him. After that, it's up to him."

"Fair enough," I said and settled in to wait.

Twenty minutes later, a man approached my table. "I hear you're looking for me."

I told him my name, then said, "Is it true you raise donkeys?"

"It is." Vazquez remained standing. "Why?"

"I may have a business proposition for you," I said. "Can I buy you breakfast?"

He removed his hat, revealing a shock of wavy black hair. He straddled the chair, his huge brown eyes smiling. My awkwardness melted away. We were about the same age. "How big is your ranch?" I said.

"Only a few acres."

My shoulders dropped. "Then you don't have many donkeys on hand?"

"I have as many or as little as I want."

"I don't understand."

Francisco laughed. "My supply is in the mountains."

"Would you sell to an individual like me?"

"Depends. Can you pay?"

I slapped my forehead. Why hadn't I thought of it earlier? I could have saved myself a lot of time. "Are there other breeders around here?"

"Sure," he said, with an impish grin. "But I'm the best."

I burst out laughing. Francisco was such an affable person that those words didn't sound conceited. "Perhaps we can do business," I said. "Can you get me one hundred now—and another hundred over the next two weeks?"

Francisco's eyes widened, then his face grew pensive. "It'll be tight, but I think we can manage. Now, let's talk money."

"I'd like to see your operation first."

"Okay—after you buy me that breakfast, amigo."

Francisco's ranch was ten miles away. When we could ride abreast, we talked. "How long you been in business, Francisco?"

"My father started it when I was four—I guess it's in my blood."

"Is he still around?"

"Died three years ago." Francisco looked over at me. "You?"

"Mine died a few years ago, too. We never had much of a relationship though. We were always struggling."

"Know what you mean." Francisco came to a halt. "There she is."

I looked down. "It looks so tiny."

"I don't need a big area, I let the donkeys roam in the wild."

"Do you actually breed them?"

Francisco laughed and started down. "You know, this is really an easy business. The jennies reproduce from age three to thirty and they're ready to entertain a male seven days after foaling. Right now, I have four hundred jennies in various stages of reproduction."

"Do you have males just for breeding?"

"Don't have to. When a jenny is ready, we tie her to one of those stakes at the base of the mountain. Her braying attracts the wild jack and voilà, we have a foal in the making—one with the tameness of the mother and the hardiness of the father."

"How old are the donkeys you're selling?"

"Around three, some maybe a little older. Working them too soon retards their growth."

"You seem to know what you're doing," I said, dismounting from my horse.

"Come on, I'll show you around."

My heart raced. I'd never seen so many donkeys—gray ones, black ones, brown ones, white ones—all in one place.

"These are ready to be shipped," he said, when we came to the fourth corral. "See any you like?"

"Wow, they look so healthy. I'm surprised you have so many."

"The last few years have been slow. Land is concentrating in the hands of a few, and they seem to work more efficiently with less animals."

I selected several and checked their teeth—the best indicator of care. "How much for a hundred?" I said.

"Three hundred a head."

"Three hundred?" I couldn't believe my ears.

"Is something wrong?"

"No. No," I said, trying to hide my surprise. "I was just wondering how I'd get them to Orizaba."

"We'll herd them to the railroad for twenty-five a head."

"It's a deal," I said, happy for the help. "What about the shipyards in Veracruz?"

"It's easy, the train takes you right there. You could do it yourself—or hire someone hanging around the docks."

"I'll take a hundred now and if all goes well, I'll be back for another fifty by week's end."

The next morning, Francisco's boys drove the donkeys to the railroad depot without a hitch. Once the animals were loaded, I bought a ticket. The train took us over cedar- and walnut-covered mountains, through coffee and tobacco plantations, and down into the hot coastal lowlands, where tropical fruit is grown.

The closer we came to Veracruz, the hotter and stickier the train became. Despite the humidity, I liked the buoyant feeling of being at sea level.

While the train switched tracks into the shipyards, I walked the beach along the Gulf of Mexico. The moist, salty air filled my lungs and I felt I could walk forever.

When the animals were safely on board, I returned to Orizaba for fifty more. "Thanks Francisco," I said. "I'll be back next week for the rest."

Once I'd seen the last of two hundred up the ship's plank the following week, I plopped down in the sand and watched the endless waves wash ashore. It was beautiful here, but I couldn't wait to get home.

While safer and more comfortable than hours in a saddle, the train ride made me feel idle. Although I enjoyed the scenery, I promised myself that next time I'd bring a book. Meanwhile, I made a list of things to do. Finding Francisco had given me a new burst of energy.

As we passed through Calpulalpan, I grew impatient. I wanted to be home. Suddenly the train jolted and came to an abrupt stop. After about an hour, the conductor walked through my car and said, "The wheel slipped off the track and cracked. We're waiting for a replacement."

"Can I get my horse?" I said, too restless to sit any longer.

Ten miles later, I came to the village of San Cristóbal. I stopped at a small café for lunch. Much to my surprise, the place was crowded. I ordered and sat listening to the scuttlebutt. These men had gathered for a reason.

Finally, one of them said to me, "Hey stranger, what would you do in our situation?"

Surprised, I said, "Why ask me? I'm not involved."

"Maybe you can give us some insight."

Feeling a bit honored now, I said, "What's the problem?"

"We're tenants on this apple orchard." The man motioned in a vague direction, then continued. "Yesterday, the owner said he's selling and he wants us off the property within the week! We have no money—nowhere to go." The man shrugged. "We're lost . . . we don't know what to do."

My stomach knotted. I wanted to run away, but I remained riveted to my chair. "What happened?" I said, finally.

"I guess the buyer wants his own crew. We could find other work—but we're being deprived of our homes. It's just not fair."

I gaped past the man at the next table, my mind flashing images of Hernandez telling me to leave. I thought I'd buried those feelings. Now the old hurt and anger blossomed.

"Señor," the man said, touching my arm. "You okay?"

I sipped some water. "You have no other income?"

"Last fall's crop was small, this year's worse."

My lunch came, but I was no longer hungry. I felt a strong bond with these men. Losing your home is devastating enough, but having to house and feed a family too? I couldn't even imagine.

"Well, Señor?" He stared at me. "What would you do?"

I toyed with my beans. Finally I said, "Can you show me the land?"

Three men eagerly volunteered.

The farmer who seemed to be the leader talked most of the way. "The owner recruited us with promises of prosperity. We sold everything to rent the land . . . now we have nothing."

"How many are you?"

"Ten families."

"Have you tried to buy the land?"

"We put all our own cash into saving the land—the owner promised to repay us."

The orchard was meager, badly in need of fertilizer and water, but I could tell it was beautiful to these men. Suddenly I understood why my father never left. He, too, loved the land. I had the power to help them. But did I want to?

After several hours of looking around, I said, "I need more information. Where can I find the owner?"

Another pulled out his pocket watch and smiled with his lips only. "Margarita's Cantina—where he always is at this hour."

I went there. Inside, I said to the bartender, "I'm looking for the owner of the apple orchard."

"Over there, in the corner," he gestured.

I went over and tapped the man's shoulder. "Excuse me, Señor. I understand you . . ."

The man turned and looked up.

My jaw tightened. "You?" I stepped back. "You own the or-chard?"

"My God, is that you . . . Juan? Yes, Juan Gomez, isn't it?"

"So—we meet again."

Hernandez glanced away and then glared back at me. "What do you want?"

"I came to talk about your land—but seeing it's you—well, I understand why you want to leave them homeless." My fists clenched. I hated him. I turned to leave.

"It's not what you think," he said.

I stopped. "You interested in selling?" I said, over my shoulder.

"I have a buyer, but he's offering less than I want."

My feet froze to the floor. Helping the farmers meant help-ing Hernandez. Yet I felt compelled to continue. "How much?" I said.

"Twenty-five thousand."

I gulped. That was a lot to risk for an orchard that may not make it. I looked at Hernandez with contempt. "I may be in-terested. I'll let you know." We set a date to meet again.

I left the bar in a daze. When I settled down a bit, I began to wonder what had happened to Hernandez. He looked awful. But I was too angry to care.

Sputtering, I walked down the street. He never gave me a chance to prove myself. He pushed my parents so hard and paid them little. Men like him were parasites, bloodsuckers.

Why should I do anything? Most likely it would be several seasons before I'd see a good crop. I'd have to advance the men a lot of money. And even that didn't guarantee the orchard's survival.

My mind did flip-flops all through that fretful night. A part of me wanted to walk away and never come back. But the other couldn't forget the farmers. Their lives reminded me so much of my own. I knew I had to do something.

Sharing the Wealth

AFTER A RESTLESS NIGHT OF WONDERING WHAT TO do, I left San Cristóbal and went to see Hector. I hoped he could help me sort through my predicament.

Miguel escorted me into the alcove, where Hector sat staring out the window. "You still sick?" I said, when I saw how little he'd eaten.

"I walked two miles this morning," he boasted. His voice sounded more upbeat than he looked.

Pouring myself a cup of coffee, I sat down. As much as I needed his words of wisdom, I wasn't going to ask for them. Hector didn't look well. We stared at each other for a long moment. Finally he said, "Did you quit?"

I nodded. "Hector, what did the doctor say?"

"I'm on the mend, these things take time." He searched my face. "Did you fulfill the contract?"

"Yes, after the idea of a donkey breeder occurred to me."

Hector smiled. "I wondered when you were going to realize it."

"You knew, why didn't you tell me?"

"That's what prosperity is all about, learning how to think creatively. You did well."

"It just took me forever," I said glumly.

"Next time it won't take so long."

I stared down at my coffee, wondering if I should tell Hector about the orchard.

"Something upsetting you?" he said.

After a deep sigh, I blurted out the whole story.

Hector shrugged. "So far, I don't see what's bothering you."

"The farmers reminded me of my past . . ." I started pacing. ". . . so I wanted to help. But when I met the owner, I wasn't so sure."

Hector raised an eyebrow. "Why's that?" he said.

"Hernandez . . ." Images of my parents, the farm, his attitude flashed through my mind. "When I saw him, all I wanted to do was hit him. I wanted to pay him back for all the hurt he caused me."

"Is this the same . . . ?"

"That awful man. Why should I help him?"

Hector watched me pace. Finally he said, "Why are you letting the past control your present?"

I stopped dead. "Me? He's the one who hasn't changed. It's time he got what's coming to him."

"Maybe he already has . . ."

"Ooh, I can't stand him, I'm . . ." I clenched my fists. "I won't do business with him."

"Why are you holding a grudge? Hernandez wasn't trying to hurt you when he asked you to leave."

"Asked?"

"All right, ordered—but he was doing only what he thought necessary for him to survive."

"Damn it, it hurts, it hurts bad—he pushed my parents until they buckled under the pressure."

"So that's it? You blame him for their deaths?"

"Yes . . . no . . . I mean . . . I don't know." My shoulders dropped. I sat down, exhausted. The tears came and I buried my head in my arms.

Finally Hector said softly, "Juan, I don't believe Hernandez meant to hurt you. And when you understand that, you'll be able to feel some compassion for him."

"Maybe," I said, wiping my eyes. They felt like sandpaper.

"All things happen for a reason. In a way, he did you a favor."

"Right, Hector," I said, rolling my eyes.

"Look where you are now compared to where you would have been had you stayed on that farm. Sometimes a greater destiny, more powerful than we can understand, takes control of our lives."

"You're saying, if I forgive him, I'll buy the apple orchard?"

"Not at all—you must do what is right and profitable in business, without letting emotions control you."

Hector licked his lips. "Go splash some cold water on your face—I'll tell Miguel to make some hot chocolate and we'll meet in the library."

I left. Somehow I had to reconcile my hatred. I had to forgive Hernandez, but I was too ashamed to tell Hector that I couldn't. Not yet anyway, and certainly not so easily. When I returned, Miguel had just left the warm chocolate milk and there was a nice fire in the fireplace.

"You look much better," Hector said.

I sat down. "So what do you think? Should I buy the orchard?"

"Land is a good investment," Hector said slowly. "It isn't instant money like selling a donkey."

"I know it's going to cost plenty and I don't know anything about apples."

"Your problem brings to mind an idea . . . ," Hector replied thoughtfully. "I call it a cooperative. The tenants become your partners. In exchange for working the land, they receive half the profits."

"Isn't that what my parents did? I don't want to be a landlord like Hernandez."

"Your father leased the land and received only a very small percentage of the profits. When he died, you had no control. In a cooperative, everyone works the land and each becomes a part-owner of the whole. The better the land does, the higher the profit."

I took a sip of my hot chocolate. "I don't know . . . half seems like a lot."

"You need to understand, Juan, owning land carries with it certain responsibilities."

"My father always said, 'Be good to the land and it'll be good to you.'"

"For you, it goes deeper than that," Hector said, getting up to stoke the fire. "You must learn to share your wealth."

"Hector," I said, fingering the pesos in my pocket. "I'm confused. First you tell me to save my money and now you're telling me to give it away. I'm afraid I'll end up with nothing."

"Slow down," he said. "What I'm saying is—use your wealth to create opportunities for others so they can better themselves."

"I don't understand," I said.

"You're not giving away the land, only half the profit, which the farmers will work hard for. In turn, they'll learn to become self-sufficient and, hopefully, never be in this predicament again."

"I don't know," I said, shaking my head. Hector was asking me to act like a rich man, when I was only the son of a poor tenant farmer. "I could go broke being so generous."

"You'll be surprised—your wealth will grow faster. But don't try anything you feel uncomfortable with . . . it may not be right for you."

"I haven't even decided to buy the land."

"Oh, haven't you?"

I stared at him, then paced pensively around the room, under the watchful eye of Carmen. Even from far away, she was stunning. "Why did you pick this room to tell me about sharing? Is it because she's in here?"

Hector fell silent. Finally he said, "Sharing is much like love. The more you give, the more you have to give."

"It's hard for me to accept this. I've had to scrimp all my life."

"Okay, tell you what—I'd like to help. Institute the cooperative and I'll pay the farmers' expenses for the first year."

"I couldn't let you do that," I said, sitting down in the wingback chair.

"It's not a gift. If the idea works, you and the farmers can repay me over three years with no interest. If it doesn't, you owe me nothing."

The offer was tempting. "How about if I keep you informed?"

"Okay, but my offer stands if you need it."

"Thanks, Hector. You're very generous."

"It's not generous. Success brings with it a duty to teach others how to make money so they'll always have it themselves. So I hope, through my example, you're learning to share your good fortune, just like I'm sharing mine."

I stood up and stretched. "It's late. You've given me plenty to think about and you look like you could use some rest, too."

The next morning, I returned to the city. First I went to Buford's office and turned in my paperwork. "One hundred are in Texas," he said. "You should have your money in three weeks."

Three weeks? I needed the money now. I hated to use up all my available cash. What if something happened. After my meeting, I rushed home. I couldn't wait to see Juanita and the boys. With happy tears, I hugged each of them.

"We missed you over the holidays," Juanita said, stirring the beans. "How was your trip?"

"Lonely. In fact, I would have been here earlier had the solution not occurred to me."

"I'm glad it worked, Juan," said José. "Pedro gave me your job—as long as you didn't want it back."

"He really misses you," Juanita said, spooning out the beans. "Sometimes he forgets and calls José, Juan."

"I'm sorry," I said to José. "That must be awful for you."

José shrugged. "I usually answer him, but I see the disappointment."

"I'll stop in and see him soon," I said. Then I turned to Carlos. "How's school?"

"Boring," Carlos said.

"I've talked to them about advancing him, but no one will listen—I'm just his mother."

"I'll try if you like—after my next business trip."

"I'm going to be the lead in our school play," Paco said, climbing into my lap. "Will you come, Juan?"

"I wouldn't miss it."

When dinner was finished, I asked the boys if I could talk to Juanita alone. "Juanita," I said. "I hope you can find it in your heart to forgive me."

She looked at me as if I'd lost my mind. "Forgive you? For what?"

"For taking you and the boys for granted."

"What are you talking about?" She sounded almost irritated.

"I've been here close to three years, doing nothing, while you gave me the warmth and security of a family. Now I think it's time I repay you."

"You've paid rent, been like a father to my boys, you owe me nothing."

"Juanita . . . ," I said, taking her hand. "They're building new apartments up by Pedro's—places with running water, toilets, electricity, police protection. I think we should move."

"Move? That's out of the question," she said. "My father lived here and his father before him."

For a moment, my head spun. She was so emphatic. I had expected Juanita to react practically, not emotionally. Finally I said, "Okay, then, let's expand your home and add all the modern conveniences."

"That'd cost too much," she said, her eyes sweeping around the room.

"It's the way of progress," I said. Although I was worried about my cash flow, I caught the flash of excitement in Juanita's eyes. "Do you know a good builder?"

"There is one . . ." Her shoulders fell. "But I can't . . ."

"Ask him to draw up some plans. We'll decide together."

Juanita squeezed my hand. There was a light in her eyes that made my heart dance. "Juan, how can I ever thank you?"

"It's me who's thanking you. You opened your heart to me when I needed it most. I'll never forget that."

Juanita's glowing face stayed with me throughout the night and on the train the next morning. When we neared Calpulalpan, Hernandez's face supplanted Juanita's and my heart began to race. I felt like the little boy who cowered in the barn every time Hernandez came to visit. After all this time, he still had a hold on me.

With each passing mile, my anxiety grew. Finally, I galloped on my horse to Margarita's Cantina. Hernandez was exactly where I'd left him. His face was drawn and he wore the same rumpled clothes. I pulled out the chair across from him and sat down.

Hernandez stared at his drink. "Contrary to popular opinion, I don't spend all my time in here getting drunk."

"I don't give a damn what you do, I'm here because of your land."

"Interesting it should end this way."

"I swore someday I'd get you . . . well, I couldn't have planned it any better."

Hernandez met my fiery gaze. "What do you care? From what I've heard you've done quite well for yourself."

I rolled my eyes. "You can't take credit for what's happened to me."

"It's merely an observation." Hernandez turned the glass in his hands. "Ironically, your father's death was a big turning point for me, too."

The mention of my dad made me feel sad. "I'm prepared to make you an offer."

Hernandez sipped his beer. "I'm not after your sympathy. Asking you to leave was strictly business."

"One handled very poorly. You left me with no resources and no dignity."

"I don't expect you to believe this, but I was afraid to become friendly. It was never easy—pushing people all the time."

"That's no excuse. My parents slaved for you."

"Yeah, well, it doesn't matter now. I did what I thought best. When I told you to leave, I had three other parcels to fill. That year's crop was dismal and I sold at a loss."

I studied Hernandez's eyes. The evil black that I always saw there was now a soft brown. Had I only imagined it—or had something changed him? "Why did you sell?"

"I thought the orchard would take less time and bring in more money. You see, my wife was ill . . ."

"How is she?" I said, surprised to see his tears.

"She died . . . two months ago." Hernandez wiped his eyes. "I thought I'd feel relieved, but I . . . she was my mainstay."

This is the man I'd been hating? "I'm sorry," I said. And I truly meant it.

My heart filled with sorrow and for a moment, I let the feeling consume me. Then I reached into my pocket and counted out twenty-five thousand pesos on the table. "I was going to bargain with you, but after hearing your story, I want to meet your price."

He signed the deed. "They're good men, Juan, you won't regret it."

"Good luck, Señor Hernandez," I said, shaking his hand. "I wish you well."

Afterward, I went looking for the farmers and found the same three huddled together in the coffee shop. "I just bought the orchard," I said, tapping the leader's shoulder.

"Congratulations," he said tentatively. "What are you going to do with it?"

"Your homes are safe," I said, smiling. "Let's meet here tomorrow at one o'clock to discuss bringing the orchard back to life."

The tension drained from his face. "We'll spread the word."

The next day, the restaurant was crowded with men, women, and children. After introducing myself, I said, "Once we've discussed our business, I'll be happy to answer any questions you have about me."

I cleared my throat and launched into Hector's idea of a cooperative farm. When I finished, a rather emaciated-looking man with a pencil-thin mustache stood up and crossed his arms. "Why should we trust you?" he said.

Taken aback, I said, "I'll put the agreement in writing if that makes you feel more secure."

"Hernandez promised us a good life, too. We accepted his offer and lost everything."

A few others nodded. "I'm offering to pay all the expenses until the orchard makes a profit."

"The other buyer was going to pay us to leave our homes. At least we'd have some money. How are we going to live under this cooperative?"

I did some quick thinking. "The idea here is not to become totally dependent on me or the orchard. Your homes are safe, but while the orchard hangs in the balance, you'll have to find some outside income."

The thin man remained standing. "What if there is no profit at the end of the first year?"

"The orchard didn't get sick overnight, and I don't expect it to get well in one season."

"Will we pay 50 percent of the supplies?"

"For now, I'll purchase everything. What I do need is a list so we can get started as soon as possible."

Another man said, "I don't always want to work for someone else. Is there any chance we'll ever own the land?"

Hector told me this issue might come up and to be prepared for it. "As of this moment, each of you owns 5 percent of the land. After one year, if you want out, we'll determine a value for your percentage and buy it from you. It'll be up to the majority if they want to let another family buy in." I paused, allowing them to absorb my words. "In addition, I'll give you the option of purchasing the orchard from me in ten years." Suddenly the place was in an uproar.

The skinny man hadn't budged. "I don't trust you," he said over the noise. "I know all about you, Donkey Man, how you were arrested for stealing."

My face felt hot. How could he possibly know that? The room was quiet. These people expected an answer. I swallowed hard. "It's true, I was arrested—it was a mistake. The manager of the auction went public and verified my story. I was never charged."

I shifted my weight. "If you want out, my good man, I'll pay you your 5 percent now. That's 1,250 pesos. And the same for anyone else." I pulled out my wallet and held it in the air in front of me.

After an awkward silence, the leader stood up. "Donkey Man, count me in." Then eight more me-toos. The thin man stood still.

"Well, Abe," the leader said. "You in or out?"

"Hell, what do I have to lose?"

At that point, the nine other men descended on him and shook his hand. Then the leader turned to me and said, "Will we be seeing much of you?"

"I'd like to spend one day a week working here."

The farmers huddled briefly, then went to speak with their wives. Again, the leader spoke. "When you come, we'd like you to rotate staying with one of us."

I broke into a big grin. My family was about to grow tenfold.

Awakening to Spiritual Wealth

AFTER THAT CHAOTIC MONTH, I ACHED FOR SOME routine in my life and got it during the next few months. Once the donkeys passed inspection in Texas, the cavalry gave me a standing order of fifty per month for eleven more months.

Manuel designed a new bracelet at the first of the year. When I showed it to the Texan, he ordered sixty per month. Manuel took the news in his typical fashion—he complained about all the hours he was working. So we renegotiated a higher price for each piece.

Juanita's home turned out beautifully. In addition to a tiled floor, we had running water, electricity, and a bathroom. We also had a kitchen separate from the living room, five bedrooms, and my office.

"Just think," Juanita said. "No more chamber pot to put out each morning for waste pickup."

Since José assumed many of my old duties at the restaurant, I hired Carlos and Paco to work for me after school. They helped me keep the accounting up-to-date.

Farmers continued to visit the restaurant looking for the Donkey Man. The staff gave people directions to my new office. Each time their assistance resulted in new business, I noted it and paid them a commission at month's end.

I traveled three to four days a week. By train, it took only a few hours to reach San Cristóbal. I spent the first night in town, and the second with one of the families. The farmers learned to trust again as they saw my plans unfold. With proper care, the orchard was beginning to look healthier. But I still didn't expect much of a crop that first year.

Every other week, I went to Francisco's. I no longer attended the auction. Instead, I shipped some of the animals back to Mexico City for eventual placement with the ranchers, while the rest went on to the cavalry in Texas.

And, of course, I stopped at Hector's whenever I could. Our relationship started because I needed guidance. And even though we grew closer after he told me about Carmen, I still thought of him as my mentor. He still called me Juan, and a part of me still considered myself the son of a poor tenant farmer. However, my name and reputation as the Donkey Man spread and I prospered.

When my life started settling down into a new routine, I realized that I was changing. But exactly how, I couldn't quite put my finger on.

One Monday morning, after Hector showed me a shortcut through his estate, I headed for San Cristóbal. My horse trotted easily over the rolling hills. The air smelled of spring and I hoped for rain. The orchard really needed a good drenching.

Suddenly I heard from the side of the road, "Excuse me, Señor . . . can you spare some water?"

My eyes fell upon on a young woman sitting up against a tree trunk. I grabbed my canteen and approached her. She had the biggest brown eyes I'd ever seen.

She moistened her dry, cracked lips. "I felt dizzy, so I left my horse and started walking."

"Can I help you home?" I said, pouring water into her cupped hands.

Shivering, she nodded. "I would be most grateful."

Leaving her my jacket and canteen, I went to get her horse. When I returned, I lifted her up into my saddle. "Which way?" I said.

Closing her eyes, she rested against me and pointed in the direction I was heading.

I stared down at her. Her face was oval, and her brows were lush and arched over long, thick, curly lashes. Her small, turned-up nose added a softness to her otherwise stern features. Her thick hair seemed too heavy for her small frame. I wondered if her personality was as sharply contrasting as her physical features.

Gently, I brushed the wisps of perspiration-soaked hair away from her face. One part of me wanted to go faster so she could get help sooner, while the other wanted to linger.

Briefly, she opened her eyes. "Next one on the left," she said.

My heart felt heavy. I didn't want her to leave me. We trudged in under a sign in the archway that read: Mendez Farm.

Her mother came running toward us. "What's happened to my Maria?" she screamed. She was soon joined by her husband and two sons.

"I found her by the side of the road. She's very ill and needs a doctor."

Without a word, the father took Maria away from me. "Papa . . . he was very kind," she said, while her mother led her into the house.

Relief spread across Mendez's face. "Please wait," he said. After instructing one of the boys to get a doctor, he, too, went inside.

Soon he returned. "She's resting . . ." He wiped the sweat from his forehead. "She was so late . . . thank you for bringing her home."

We shook hands. That's it, we just say good-bye? But Señor, I wanted to scream, I want, no *need* to see Maria again. But my throat froze. Instead, I got on my horse and continued on my way as if nothing had happened.

But the next day at the orchard and the next at Francisco's, I conducted my business in a daze. I couldn't stop thinking about Maria. "What's the matter, Donkey Man?" people asked. "It's just spring fever," I said.

From Francisco's, we transported seventy donkeys to the railroad yard—fifty were earmarked for Veracruz and twenty for Mexico City. I later learned that only nineteen arrived in the city alive.

Because I had to replace that donkey, I planned my weekend so I could attend the auction on Saturday and easily stop and see Maria on Sunday.

At the auction, there were many acceptable animals to choose from, so I planned to buy the first one that came up for bid and go home.

Inside, a wiry young man with an open smile sat down next to me. "Good evening, Señor," he said. "Great night for an auction."

I returned his smile. "It seems people agree with you. This place is packed."

When the auction started, the kid next to me bid aggressively on every donkey, then stopped, and never won any of them. "Is this your first time?" I said, during a lull.

"My boss will be so angry . . . ," he said, shaking his head. "He gave me only three hundred pesos."

"Three hundred won't buy anything tonight."

Tears filled the boy's eyes. "I'll probably lose my job."

Just then, the next animal came up for bid. It was the one I wanted. I won it for three hundred seventy-five pesos. When I was handed the slip to pay the cashier, I smiled at the boy, feeling a bit superior. I could buy any donkey I wanted. "It was nice meeting you," I said.

For a moment, the boy looked crestfallen. Then he turned his attention to the next donkey up for bid.

After paying for my animal, I started to go get it. But instead, I went back to my seat. "Here," I said, handing the kid the bill of sale.

The kid looked confused. "I can only pay three hundred."

"You keep it," I said. "Good luck."

The kid stood up. "What about you?"

I shrugged. "I'll get the next one."

"Thank you, Señor, thank you very much." Then he ran to claim his prize.

The next day, I traveled the long route to Hector's, hoping to see Maria on the way. Just being near her house again left me trembling. My heart pounded with memories of her as I stepped up to the entryway. I wiped my sweaty palms on my pants, then knocked on the door.

"Good afternoon, Señora Mendez," I said, taking off my hat. "Remember me—Juan Gomez—I . . . I brought Maria home last Monday."

"Oh, yes. *Yes.*" She smiled and invited me in. "Can I get you something cold to drink?"

"I came about Maria. How is she?"

The woman shook her head. "She's still very sick."

"Señora, would it be all right if I came back next week to check on her?"

"Sure, sure," she said. "I'll tell Maria you stopped by."

I opened the door and sprang toward my horse. My heart soared. Maybe I hadn't seen Maria, but I had permission to return. What more could I hope for? On my way to Hector's, I sang right along with the birds in the warm spring sunshine. The earth was blossoming and so was I.

Hector was mulching his flower garden when I rode up. "Why are you so radiant?" he said.

I got down from my horse, blushing. "How can you tell I have news before I say anything?"

Hector threw back his head and laughed. "She must be very special," he said.

My mouth dropped open. "How'd you . . . ?"

"Miguel, Miguel! Bring the brandy," he said, passing through the kitchen.

Miguel poured us each a shot in the alcove. "To new love," Hector toasted. Our glasses clinked.

The brandy went down, leaving a warm trail. I felt light-headed. "Her name's Maria and she's beautiful."

"That's a good start. How'd you meet?"

"I found her sitting by the side of the road, she was ill and I took her home. God." I ran my fingers through my hair. "What if she won't have anything to do with me?"

"Does the family know who you are?"

"No! In fact, Mendez offered to pay me for helping her. I turned him down, of course."

"Going out of your way to help others is a good philosophy to live by. Even though you may not be rewarded financially, the spiritual rewards are great."

"I'd have done the same for anyone. Meeting Maria was an added bonus."

Hector nodded. "It's nice to go to sleep at night knowing you've been of service to someone else."

I leaned back in my chair. "So that's what's been happening to me lately?" I remembered the excitement in making Juanita happy, giving the farmers some security, letting go of my hatred for Hernandez, and helping the boy at the auction. "Doing things for others has made me feel so good."

Hector beamed. "You know Juan, money is only one aspect of true wealth. If you continue to apply the lessons I've been teaching, spiritual wealth will naturally follow."

"Wealth of spirit," I said, delighted. "Yes. It's a feeling, a glow, that's coming from the core of me."

"You're discovering that there is an order to life. And, as you integrate your financial and spiritual wealth, every aspect of your life will benefit."

"How so?"

"To name a few: you'll be happier, healthier, kinder, more generous, more considerate."

"I like this feeling. I'll have to look for new situations. New ways to help people."

"You do that," Hector said. "But as you grow wealthier, re-member to help the people who've helped you along the way."

"I'd like to do something more for Juanita, I just don't know what."

"My impression is she's a proud woman," Hector said. "Whatever you decide, present it in such a way so it doesn't feel like charity."

Miguel announced dinner. Before Hector took his first bite, he said, "How old is Maria?"

"Eighteen, maybe. It must sound silly, me feeling the way I do, when I don't know much about her."

"Feelings aren't logical." Hector's eyes took on a nostalgic look. "I felt that way about Carmen."

"If she's well enough, maybe I'll know more on Sunday." We continued eating in silence. "Hector, I hope this isn't too painful for you," I said, finally.

Hector shook his head. "Seeing you like this brings back some wonderful memories. I hope it works out for you."

"Me too," I said. But I had no idea what to expect. All I knew was that Maria occupied a good portion of my every waking moment.

Respect and Emotional Wealth

T HAT NEXT WEEK PASSED LIKE AN ETERNITY. I
canceled my trip to the orchard because the donkey
business needed attention. After wiring Francisco my
weekly order, I sat down with a map to plan my schedule.

On Saturday night, I went to Hector's. We had decided the
week before to get together a day early so I could rest up before visiting Maria. After Hector went to bed, I sat outside
looking at the stars, wondering what it'd be like to see her
again. Would I be disappointed? Maybe she wouldn't remember me.

The next morning, I took the shortcut through Hector's
estate. Once at the Mendez farm, I stomped up the front
path and knocked on the door. My insides shook. I waited.
And waited. I was about to knock again when the door
opened. It was her, looking more beautiful than I remembered.

"Please come in, Señor Gomez."

"Call me Juan," I said, returning her radiant smile. "I just
stopped by to see how you're feeling." Like the week before, I
stepped just inside the door.

Maria grabbed my arm and pulled me into the kitchen.
"I'm very well . . . thanks in part to you, Juan. Stay and have
something to eat with us?"

I stared down at her hand touching my arm. Our eyes met.

Self-consciously, she let go. "Well? Can you stay?"

Stifling an urge to say will you marry me, I finally said,
"I'd love to . . . if I'm not imposing."

Frantically, I glanced around the kitchen. I needed to focus on something other than Maria if I hoped to keep my feelings a secret. Walking over to the woodstove, I drew in a deep breath. "Is that molé sauce I smell?"

Señora Mendez spooned some out. "Would you like a taste?"

I slurped the hot liquid. "Mmmm," I said. "Just the right amount of cinnamon and chocolate."

"A man who knows about cooking?" The Señora raised her eyebrows. "Where did you learn?"

"In a restaurant."

"A cook?"

I shook my head. "A waiter. And cook's sampler. I could always tell what was missing."

"We're not having anything fancy right now. But come next week for something special."

My heart did somersaults. "Thank you, I'd like that." I spotted Maria carrying a full tray. "Can I help?" I offered.

"Take this into the dining room. Mama and I will bring the food."

In a matter of seconds, I set the table just like I'd learned at Pedro's.

Señor Mendez walked in. "Who did this to the table?"

"Doesn't it look beautiful?" Maria said. "Juan works in a restaurant."

Before I could say anything, Mendez pulled out his chair and sat down. "You city boys are all alike. Don't know what hard work is all about."

The statement left me cold. What did Mendez know about how rough I'd had it? "I grew up on a farm, Señor," I said, hoping to show him we had something in common.

Mendez sat back and crossed his arms. "Why did you leave? Not man enough to stay and help?"

I stared at him. Maybe he's possessive and suspicious of any man who's interested in his daughter. I swallowed hard and looked at Maria. "My parents died, I had no choice."

"Did you bail out like all the others and sell to the plantations?"

"Papa, that's enough," Maria said. "Juan is our guest."

"I don't mind," I said. "The truth is, Señor, I wanted to stay but the landlord wouldn't let me. You see, I was all alone . . ."

"We grow chilies here," Señora Mendez said proudly. "That's what adds to the molé . . . fresh chilies."

Her comment snapped the tension. Throughout the rest of the meal, we talked about farming, cooking, the weather. I relaxed a little and tried not to look at Maria, because when I did, my eyes stayed glued to hers. I wanted so much to hold her again.

When I got ready to leave, Señora Mendez said at the door, "See you next Sunday."

"Maria?" I said, while we strolled down the path. "I . . . I've been wondering . . . well . . . you don't have to answer if you don't want to."

She touched my arm lightly. "What is it?"

"Why aren't you married?" I said, hoping to get information that might give me an edge.

"I've had proposals, but Papa turned them all down."

"Don't you have any say?"

"I guess I didn't care that much." She stopped and smiled up at me.

"What kind of man would your father accept?"

Maria thought for a moment. "There is someone," she said. "I've heard the men talking . . . They all seem to admire what he's accomplished. Papa said I'd be lucky to find an honorable man like that."

"Who is he?"

Maria shrugged. "I don't remember his name."

"How do you know of him?"

"Relatives in San Cristóbal." Maria's eyes sparkled like diamonds. "They said he bought an apple orchard—put all his money on the line—and then gave the land back to ten families."

Oh no, I thought. She's talking about me. But what an exaggeration. Not even Hector would be that generous. How could I compete with such a rumor?

"I'm trying to think of his name," she said. "It seems like it was an odd name . . . donkey . . . something or other."

"Maria," I said, taking both of her hands. "I'm . . . I'm . . ."

"Yes?"

I bit my lip. "I'm . . . glad you're feeling better."

Her eyes danced. "I haven't had a chance to properly thank you."

I wanted to kiss her. "Just seeing you well is thanks enough." Climbing on my horse, I felt depressed. I wanted her to love *me*, not some inflated image of me. If I told her who I was, would she be intimidated by my money? The only way to ensure that wouldn't happen was to get her to fall in love with me first, then tell her.

~

Hector was out on the front veranda when I rode up. As soon as he saw me, he stood in anticipation, then frowned. "What's the matter? Didn't it go well?"

I mustered a smile. "I've been invited back next Sunday."

"Splendid," Hector said. "Why the long face?"

"She's already infatuated—with the Donkey Man."

"I'm confused," Hector said, sitting down. "Doesn't she know?"

The sun ducked behind a cloud, making everything look just like I felt—gloomy. "She and her father have an image of me that's larger than life."

"I understand how difficult it is to live up to one's reputation, but . . ."

"Maybe I'll just go into hiding, too."

"Juan, for you it's different. You love her."

"Different for me? Why?"

"Because until you tell her, you're going to feel guilty and that will overshadow your relationship and affect your life."

"In what way?" I said, feeling somewhat confused.

"I'm not sure it's the right time. I want you to realize it on your own."

"Realize what? That I have to tell her who I am? I know that. It's just that I want her to love me—Juan Gomez."

"All the more reason to be honest."

I tore at my hair. "What's the use, her father doesn't like me anyway."

"It doesn't matter. *Your* life will never be quite right until they know everything."

"Why not?" I said, starting to pace.

"It has to do with emotional wealth."

I stopped. "What do you mean?"

"Emotional wealth encompasses a genuine respect for everything around you. It's a love of the world and of all humankind as well as a love of self."

"How do I become emotionally wealthy?"

"By recognizing that you have a choice about how you're going to behave. It's attaining a level of maturity where you consider what effect your actions have on other people. Ultimately, you try to create harmony in your life as well as in the lives of others."

I closed my eyes, hoping to hold in the tears. "What's the use? If I told him now, he'd probably never let me marry her."

"Give him time. You've only met him twice."

"He strikes me as close-minded. I'm sure he's made up his mind about me and he'll never change it."

"What makes you say that? I'd think he'd be anxious to see her married."

"Maybe—but not to me." The sun had set in a sea of reds and purples. "He's a hard-working man—has one hundred acres but farms only fifty. You won't believe what he said when I asked him why—he just shrugged his shoulders and said, 'I don't know what to do with the rest.' His attitude is a mystery to me. I could never be like that."

"Juan, if you continue to judge others, you'll never be happy." Then Hector laughed heartily. "Besides, it's taken you several years to learn a better way. You must be patient with those who haven't yet learned what you have."

"Sorry, I didn't mean to sound like a know-it-all."

"Sometimes people are afraid to take chances. They see only certain ways to make money, or they just don't know any better," Hector said. "Chilies are familiar to Mendez and he isn't about to venture away from them. You know, Juan, your Señor Mendez will never be a rich man."

"I don't care. I want to marry his daughter anyway."

"Then you need to be honest with them."

At the moment, I didn't know how to tell Maria and I had a headache from thinking about it. Hector and I took a brisk walk in the cool May night air before retiring. His place had such a calming effect on me that I slept until mid-morning. But as soon as I started for home, the nagging thoughts of Maria returned.

In my office, I read all the notes left by Paco and Carlos. I didn't want to be there. I hated the great Donkey Man. He was, after all, only the son of a poor tenant farmer. He had ignored his friends and family—all in the name of business. And now he had a reputation that I could never live up to.

After working on a few accounts, I got up and left. Eventually, I stopped at Pedro's for a late lunch and hopefully a visit with Juanita.

I walked directly into the kitchen. When Juanita saw me, she dropped her big spoon into the oversize pot. "It's been a long time," she said.

"I know," I said, embracing her. "Can you take a break?"

"In a few minutes. How long you here?"

"Just tonight. I want to spend some time with the boys later."

"They'll like that."

"Me, too," I said, breathing in the splendid aromas. Suddenly I was hungry. I walked into the dining room and ordered some *carne asada*—my favorite.

While I was finishing, Pedro approached my table. I stood up and shook hands with him. This was the first time I'd seen him since I'd quit. "It's good to see you, Pedro."

"Come to ask for your old job back—have you?"

I laughed. "Life certainly was easier then."

"I'm sorry I tried to talk you out of leaving. It'd have been a big mistake."

"You had my best interests at heart."

Pedro sat down with a heavy sigh.

"You okay?"

"I'm very tired, Juan," he said. "I'm thinking about selling."

Pedro and his restaurant were an institution in Mexico City. "What're you going to do?"

"It's the stress of these sixteen-hour days," Pedro said, mopping his brow.

"Why don't you hire a good manager?"

"You know me . . . I'm like a mother hen . . . it's best for my blood pressure if I sell."

I stared at him in disbelief. "You're really serious, aren't you?"

Pedro sat twirling his mustache. Suddenly, his eyes began to dance. "Why don't *you* buy this place?"

"*Me?* I have enough trouble keeping track of donkeys."

"Juanita and José could manage it for you. José has a real knack for this business."

"Is that so?" I leaned back in my chair. "Let me think about it."

Just then, Juanita walked up. "Am I interrupting?"

Pedro stood and offered her his chair. "Nice to see you again, Juan."

"I'll talk to you soon," I said and smiled at Juanita.

Suddenly she leaned forward, examining my face. "You've met someone, haven't you?"

I blushed. "What makes you say that?"

"Something's different . . . a certain glow," she said, her dark eyes twinkling.

Finally I admitted, "All right, all right—yes. But tell me something, Juanita. What attracts you to a man?"

"Lots of things. Kindness. Generosity. Consideration— having him be genuinely interested in me."

I sat back truly amazed. Juanita was describing someone Hector would call spiritually wealthy. I wondered if Maria was looking for the same qualities.

"Oh, yes, and above all," Juanita continued, "I value honesty."

I winced and decided not to ask what she would do if someone misled her. I couldn't face the answer. "Has there been anyone since your husband?"

"When he died . . . ," Juanita said sadly, "a part of me went with him."

I nodded. Losing my parents was tough, but losing a spouse . . . raising a family alone. "I'm sorry," I said.

Just then, the waiter came around again. I ordered another cup of coffee. "How do you like the restaurant business?"

"José makes it very exciting . . . he has so many creative ideas."

"Pedro told me." After a brief pause, I said, "He told me he wants to sell."

Juanita nodded. "I know. It's hard to think about working for someone else."

"Pedro thinks I should buy . . ." My fingertips started drumming on the table.

Juanita's eyes lit up. "José and I would be happy to run it for you."

"I was thinking . . . maybe . . . you should run it for yourselves."

"Absolutely not!" Juanita slammed her hand on the table. "You've done too much already."

"But Juanita, this would make you independent."

"I can't let you do it. We could never repay you."

"When you took me in, you gave me a family. I can never repay you."

"All I offered was a roof over your head."

"Come on, you gave me a home filled with warmth and kindness. And now I'm in a position to help you."

"Juan, it's too much . . . I just can't accept it," Juanita said, getting up to leave.

"Okay, okay," I said, grabbing her hands. Hector had said to respect Juanita's pride. "How about we split the profits fifty-fifty? I'll also set you up with 25 percent ownership, and as time goes on, your share will increase."

"That I could live with," she said, nodding.

I spent the next two days analyzing Pedro's books. After talking to Juanita and José, I met with my banker. I presented Pedro with a fair offer that he immediately accepted.

Juanita and the boys would take possession the first of July.

Foresight

HE REST OF THAT WEEK, I ROAMED THE MARKETS
looking for a gift to take to Maria. On Sunday, when I
handed her the package, I blushed.

Maria tore open the box. "Mama, look," she said, draping
the white lace shawl over her shoulders. "It's beautiful, Juan.
Thank you." She twirled around. "I'm going to show Papa."

After Maria left, the Señora stared at me. I wondered if I
had done something wrong. Uncomfortable, I offered to set
the table.

After dinner, Maria and I walked in the yard. "You talk
about farming as if you really enjoyed it," Maria said.

"Actually, I like the land." Owning it. This would be a good
time to tell her. "Maria . . ." The blood drained from my face.

"What's wrong?"

"I . . . was thinking about my parents."

"I'm sorry, Juan. What did you do after they died?"

I stopped to smell a white carnation. Another missed opportunity. "These are beautiful."

"Thank you," she said. "This is my garden."

I smiled. Hector would love her. "Have you thought about
selling them?"

"I'd much rather sell my designs," she said, pointing to her
blouse.

I looked up, surprised. "My mom used to embroider. She
sold her work in the Pachuca zócalo."

"Someday, I'd like to see the different designs in Mexico
City."

"I'll be happy to show you around."

"I'd like that, but Papa doesn't have time to take me, and I can't go alone."

The mention of her father made me uneasy. "We'll work something out." I pulled out my pocket watch. "When can I see you again?"

"How about next Sunday—for dinner." We arrived at the gate and held hands briefly. "Thanks again for that beautiful shawl," she said, smiling.

"I hope your mother didn't think it too forward of me."

"Don't worry about it," she said. "Mama likes you."

I felt dizzy with excitement traveling home. She said her mom liked me. She held my hand and asked me to come back. Once the excitement of the moment died down, however, I realized that what I wanted was happening. Maria was beginning to care. But at the same time, it was getting harder to tell her who I was.

In the following weeks, my life became a new routine. Maria's on Sundays, and thinking about her the rest of the week. Unable to concentrate on business, I browsed the markets looking for gifts.

On the one hand, I was delighted to be in love with her. On the other, I worried about her reaction when I finally told her the truth. Hector had said I would be consumed by guilt. While that hadn't happened yet, my dilemma was causing me quite a bit of concern.

The last time I was there, Maria grabbed my arm when I walked in. "It's so nice to see you, Juan," she said.

She looked so playful, her hair hanging loosely about her shoulders. I smiled and handed her a box of chocolates.

At the dinner table that day, the Señor glared at me like I was a disease that wasn't going to go away. Finally he said, "Juan, what exactly do you do for a living?"

"I'm a waiter at Pedro's Restaurant in Mexico City." As soon as I said it, I wanted to kick myself.

Mendez looked as though he didn't believe me. "How can you afford—"

"Then you must know him," Maria interrupted.

"Who?" I said.

"The Donkey Man, silly."

My last mouthful of food sat like a rock in the middle of my chest. "Why would I know him?"

"It's in today's paper." Maria pushed her chair away from the table. "He bought Pedro's."

Although outwardly I stayed calm, my insides were quaking.

"Right here," she said, pointing to the article. "It says he bought Pedro's for his friends so they would never be dependent on anyone again." Maria fell back into her chair.

I wanted to scream—that's not entirely true. Instead I said, "That happened before I started working there."

"But he owns the place, you must've seen him."

"I know who he is . . ." I looked down at my half-eaten food. For me, dinner was finished.

Maria handed me the article. It said the new owners were taking possession in two days. How long had I been out of touch?

Dabbing the napkin at my mouth, I said, "I really must be going."

Maria walked me out. "Did I say something to upset you? Will I see you next Sunday?"

"Probably not," I said. "I don't know my schedule."

"I'll miss you," she said.

I pulled her close and kissed her. When we let go of each other, Maria looked as stunned as I felt. "I love you," I whispered.

All the way back to town, Maria's kiss stayed with me. A part of me felt happy, while another felt sad. Would I lose her when she found out the truth? Hector's right. This one thing is going to nag at me and overshadow everything until I straighten it out.

At home, I met Carlos and Paco on their way out. "Mom's hosting a farewell party for Pedro at the restaurant tonight," Carlos said.

Paco went running back into the house and returned holding a small envelope. "It must be important. A man riding in a carriage delivered it."

I turned the envelope over in my hand. "What time is the party?"

"It's already started. You going to come?"

"In a little while," I said, staring at the envelope. I walked into my office and sat down. The beautifully scripted ivory envelope said: Señor Juan Gomez. I pulled out the matching card and read:

> The Dominguez Art Auction requests your presence for a private showing of original, collectible pottery and paintings. We have reserved 10 o'clock, Monday, July nineteenth, as your special time. Invited guests are to meet in front of the festival headquarters building and bring their invitations.
>
> All items not sold at the pre-showing will be offered in a general auction on Saturday evening, July twenty-fourth.

I marked the date on my calendar, remembering Hector and all his art objects. Maybe I wouldn't like anything, but it couldn't hurt to look.

After changing clothes, I went to the restaurant. Carlos met me. "I didn't have a chance to tell you earlier," he said. "Paco and I . . . we've lost orders. I told people you've been ill, but some of them were just too angry about the slow service."

"I'll have to repair the damage." My eyes glanced around the room. Juanita came in from the kitchen and spotted me at exactly the same moment. Mesmerized, I walked toward her. "Juanita, is that you?" I said, taking her outstretched hands. "You look wonderful."

Her eyes danced. "It didn't take much, a haircut, some clothes that fit."

"Remarkable," I said. Juanita's hair hung around her shoulders and flowed like water. Her red and white dress was perfect for her skin tone. "I guess you won't be hiding behind the pots anymore."

Glowing, Juanita took my arm and led me into the redesigned kitchen. "Look what José did. It cost very little and now we have room for two cooks."

I smiled. "Who's going to replace the best cook in town?"

"I've been training two men."

We walked back into the dining room. "I suppose you have plans for in here too."

Juanita grinned. "That'll have to wait until we've made some money."

"I can't believe how good you look, it makes me feel so happy."

Tears gathered in her eyes. "I didn't realize how dead I'd been until I started tackling this challenge. I can't thank you enough."

José called Juanita to help supervise the food line, so I went to find Pedro. He was circled by a crowd of well-wishers. When he saw me, he shook my hand and placed his arm around my shoulder.

"No regrets?" I said.

"The doctor said my blood pressure's already down."

I couldn't imagine Pedro inactive. "What're you going to do?"

"I'm coming back—part-time. It's worked out so well. I can't think of anyone I'd rather have own this place."

"I'm glad," I said, patting him on the back. "At least we'll be seeing you." I said good-bye to Juanita and went home. Although exhausted, I felt pretty good about my role in helping Juanita and Pedro.

My buoyant feelings disappeared when I saw the mountain of paperwork in my office. Near the top, I found a telegram from the apple orchard that said:

Urgent! STOP. Need supplies. STOP. Please come immediately. STOP.

The telegram was already a week old. I had wanted to spend some time with Juanita and the boys, but now I had to leave first thing in the morning. Those families probably felt abandoned again.

After packing a few things, I returned to my office. There were new orders, cancellations, installments and bracelets that needed collecting, and a letter from Hector. I felt embarrassed. It was time to straighten out my life. After I got my business back in shape, I was going to tell Maria and face the consequences.

Juanita and the boys came home exhausted. I told them about the emergency. "Is there anything you need before I go?"

Still glowing, Juanita said, "We're all set." She gave me a big hug and went off to bed.

I finished making my list for Paco and Carlos and went to sleep. In the morning, I caught the first train and went to the orchard. Word of my arrival spread like wildfire. Everyone gathered. "We thought we lost you," said the leader.

"Too much going on," I said. "What needs to be done?"

After a quick briefing, they handed me a list of supplies, which I went out and bought. I also set up an account, so in the future, the men could charge what they needed.

After working there three days, I left for Veracruz. It took four days to pick out my animals and get them on the ship. Then I returned to the orchard for another week.

That following Sunday, I wanted to see Maria, but I went to Manuel's instead. He was training a young man. "Are the bracelets ready?" I said.

Manuel pulled down the bundles.

"Your people are improving," I said, scanning the jewelry.

"We work hard."

"Manuel, I've been thinking," I said, picking up a bracelet. "Can you design a ring to match this?"

"Sure," Manuel said, with his toothless grin.

"If you have a sample ready by Thursday, I'll present it to our buyer."

"You will have it, Señor . . . but before you order we have to talk pesos."

I laughed. I knew it was time for another raise.

The whole next week, I delivered donkeys and collected installments due. It was a grueling job but I kept reminding myself that my reward was to see Maria on Sunday. I returned Thursday night and met with the Texan on Friday. When I showed him the ring, he bought the prototype. He wanted to show it to the people who bought the matching bracelet.

Sunday finally came and I rode out to Maria's. "You're just in time for dinner," Señora Mendez said.

Maria heard my voice and came running into the kitchen. "Here, I brought you this," I said.

Maria accepted the box. "You're spoiling me," she said. Slowly, she unwrapped the package while watching me. When she lifted the lid, her eyes grew large. "Where did you find these?"

"At the market." Actually, I'd scoured every market in every town I'd been in. They were the most unusual threads I could find.

"Thank you, Juan," she said. "These will make the most colorful designs."

When I walked into the living room, Señor Mendez ignored me. Finally, from behind the newspaper, he said, "I wonder how a waiter can afford to buy my daughter such expensive gifts."

I lowered my head. Finally I said, "The city has all kinds of unique items—if you know where to shop."

Mendez flapped down a corner of the paper and glared at me. "And the money," he added.

At dinner, Mendez glared at me more than once. Finally he said, "Where did you say you worked?"

After I told him, he clucked disapprovingly.

Dinner at Maria's was the first chance I'd had in several weeks to relax. But in a way, I couldn't wait to get home. The art showing was Monday morning and I wanted to attend.

As usual, Maria walked me out. "He doesn't like me, does he?"

"Papa has a lot on his mind. Yesterday his donkey went lame."

"Why doesn't he get another?"

"We can't afford the fifteen hundred pesos right now."

Why doesn't he look outside his own neighborhood? At that moment, my future father-in-law didn't seem too bright. But Hector would say I was being judgmental and impatient. Then I thought, this could be my perfect opportunity. I kissed her lightly on the lips. "Until next week, okay?"

On Monday, I was escorted from the fairgrounds to a secluded building on a quiet street. A man dressed in a tuxedo ushered me in.

"I'm the only one here?" I said.

"Señor," he said, "the next two hours have been reserved only for you."

I felt flattered. "I know very little about art," I said.

"Pick what you like. They're all originals." He handed me a brochure. "The price listed is our absolute minimum."

"Why me?" I said, furrowing my brow and thinking I'm just the son of a poor tenant farmer.

"We know you don't own any art—so we devised this introductory offer."

"Suppose I wait until the auction?"

"That's your choice, of course. But the pieces you like—if they aren't already sold—will go for a higher price."

I nodded and began browsing. I'd become well acquainted with the unpredictability of auctions.

Using the brochure as a reference, I marked thirty pieces of interest. With some encouragement from my host, I purchased all of them at a price I thought a little steep. But, based on his advice, I expected to get an excellent return on my investment.

He wrote up an invoice. "We'll schedule them for delivery tomorrow afternoon. You can pay the driver then."

I left the money with Paco and Carlos and then went to win back my canceled donkey orders. While in the area, I stopped to see Hector.

"I was beginning to wonder if something happened to you. Didn't you get my note?"

I'd forgotten all about it. "My life's been a daze."

"Young love?"

"I let everything go. I've spent the last few weeks playing catch-up."

"How's the romance coming?"

"Everyone seems to like me but her father," I said, shaking my head. "I guess I don't blame him."

"You haven't told them yet?"

"I plan to tell them next Sunday." I ran my fingers through my hair. "I'm so afraid of losing her."

"I hope you find the courage soon. Lies have a way of catching up with you."

"Could we talk about something else? Please."

Hector smiled his fatherly smile. "Can you stay? I'd like to go riding tomorrow."

The following morning, we rode to the northern edge of his estate. After traveling through acres of forested land, we came to a small settlement. "Hector," I said, "why is this town here, in the middle of nowhere?"

Hector gave me an impish grin. "Foresight, my boy, foresight."

"What's that?" I asked.

"Foresight is the ability to look around and draw conclusions about what is most likely to happen. Successful, wealthy people develop a sixth sense—a creative ability to see—and then have the courage to act accordingly."

"What does that have to do with this town?"

"All roads—north, south, east, and west—lead through here. It's a good day's journey to the nearest city. That's why this two-block town consists mainly of hotels, restaurants, and shops."

"You own this place?"

"I bought the land and built the buildings. The people pay me 30 percent of their profits."

"But why here?"

"I expect it to become a main thoroughfare. I'm also counting on the railroad."

"I can see a lot of growth for my donkey business with the railroad . . . it makes outlying areas closer—but it could also make my business obsolete."

"Good," Hector said. "Seeing the contingencies can help you plan."

"What do you mean?"

"Take this town. It either thrives and takes on a life of its own or, hopefully, the railroad buys the land from me. Or maybe both—but whatever happens, I'm prepared."

"What makes you so sure?"

Hector pulled out a map and showed me what he thought was the logical progression of the railroad. "If I were you, I'd purchase land on the outskirts of these towns. With the railroad running, their populations will grow tremendously—and that'll make your land very valuable."

"Right now, I'm not sure I have the money."

"Not sure?" Hector said. "Aren't you putting aside a certain percentage for investing each time you get paid?"

"Not exactly."

Hector stopped. "You need to know at all times how much cash you have available so when an opportunity presents itself, you won't drain your resources."

"It doesn't matter much. I'm in between investments now."

"On the contrary, Juan. You can't invest effectively or help others if you don't have enough to even help yourself."

"I see," I said. "That way I'll know if I can afford a particular investment."

"Exactly," Hector said. His horse started moving again. "And, in the meantime, you'll be building your investment account."

We rode into town and had lunch. "What will you do with the money if the railroad buys your land?"

"If I realize a profit, I'll split it fifty-fifty with the twenty families."

"That could be a lot of money."

Hector shrugged. "So what? I have more now than I could possibly spend."

I truly admired Hector. He had so much, was interested in acquiring more, yet delighted in sharing. I hoped that someday I'd be as generous.

On Wednesday, I returned to the city and opened another bank account. Now I had one for retirement, one for investing, and one to cover general expenses. Hector was right. This plan would considerably simplify my financial life.

Now knowing exactly how much cash I had available, I tried to find out if an art auction had been scheduled. To the best of my knowledge, it never occurred. I felt a little disappointed because depending on what was left, I may have bought more. With the pieces on display in my office, the boys had already sold three of them at a tidy profit. Perhaps I'd shown some foresight in purchasing them.

On Sunday, I visited the Mendez farm, feeling both excited and scared. Today was the day. I planned to tell them no matter what.

As usual, Maria escorted me into the living room, where her father was reading the paper. "Papa," she said. "Juan's here."

Glancing over the top of his paper, he nodded and said, "Gomez."

His greeting turned my blood to ice. "Señor," I said, wringing my hands. "I brought you something."

"You may be winning my wife and daughter over with your fancy gifts, but I assure you, I'm not so easily swayed." Then he paused. "Well, where is it?"

"Outside. I can't bring it in."

Mendez folded the newspaper and slammed it on the table. Standing, he pulled his trousers over his bulging belly. "Let's see this present of yours."

Maybe I'd made a mistake. What if he rejected my gift?

Once out the door, he said, "What's that doing there?" He pointed to the donkey next to my horse.

"It's yours, Señor. I brought it for you."

He stopped abruptly, his tone softening. "How'd you know?"

"Maria told me last week."

He shook his head. "I can't afford it."

"Señor, it's a gift."

"What did you pay for him?"

"Three hundred fifty pesos."

"How can you afford . . . ?"

Now. Tell him now. I licked my lips and took a deep breath. "Pedro's is a fine restaurant. I make good tips," I said.

Mendez looked at me, then back at the donkey. He seemed genuinely touched. "You don't know how badly . . ."

The grateful look on his face was not much different from many of my customers. "I think I do," I said, smiling. "Because I'm the Donkey . . ."

But Mendez was already on his way to the house, yelling for his family to come and see his new animal.

Later, when Maria and I were alone, she said, "Thanks for what you did. It's like a great burden's been lifted off Papa."

The sweet smell of flowers was heavy in the air. "Where'd he go?"

She smiled tenderly. "Working his new donkey."

"Maria," I said, putting my arm around her. "I'd do anything for you, I love you so much."

She nuzzled her head into the crook of my arm. "I love you, too," she said. "I wait for these quiet moments alone with you."

I gazed into her hypnotic eyes. "Then let's make it permanent."

"Juan Gomez, are you proposing to me?"

"Yes. *Yes!* Maria, will you marry me?"

Maria threw her arms around my neck and kissed me wholly on the lips. After a euphoric moment, she pulled away and frowned. "Have you asked Papa?"

"Not yet. Will he object?"

"He hasn't said anything, but I think he has some reservations about you."

"I'll ask him next week. Maria, I have something important to tell . . ."

"When shall we have the wedding—December?" She picked a white flower and put it in her hair.

"Five months? That seems like an eternity," I said, stroking her long black hair. "How about next month?"

Maria laughed. "What were you going to say?"

I looked at her glowing face. "It's not important—but this is," I said, pulling her close. I closed my eyes. My courage had dissolved again. I certainly didn't feel like a man who'd just had a marriage proposal accepted.

Going home, my horse emulated my mood. We moved slowly down the highway, our heads lowered. The darkening sky sunk my spirits even lower. I had done something nice for Maria and her father. But instead of feeling good about it, I felt terrible. All I could dwell on was how I had failed again to tell them who I was.

How could I be so smart in some ways and so dumb in others?

Learning about Truth

By Monday, I still didn't feel any better. I caught the train to San Cristóbal, worked in the orchard on Tuesday, and thought about stopping to see Maria on Wednesday. But fear got the best of me. I returned home instead.

While walking down the hallway to my office, I heard Carlos say, "You're in luck, Señor, the Donkey Man's here today."

I strolled in and came to a dead halt. "Carlos," I said. "Leave us, will you?"

Carlos glanced from me to the stranger. "Is everything all right?"

"Yes," I said, staring at the visitor.

"You . . . You're the Donkey Man?"

I closed my eyes and let out a deep sigh.

"I'm confused," he said, grabbing the back of the chair. "I went to Pedro's looking for Juan Gomez."

"Please sit down, can I get you something to drink?"

"It all fits," he said, after a brief pause. "I don't know if I should punch you or feel relieved."

"Probably punching me would make us both feel better."

He sat down, patting his hand over his heart. "My Maria? Why haven't you told her?"

Another deep sigh. "I've wanted to—tried to . . . she holds the Donkey Man in such awe . . ."

"I knew you had too much money. I thought you were a bandido."

"Well, I'm glad you know. I've been wondering how . . . I want to marry her. I'd like your blessing."

"Son," Mendez said, mopping his forehead. "I'd be honored to have you in the family . . ."

My breathing came easier.

"But my Maria—she values honesty."

"Señor," I said. "I didn't tell her because I was afraid."

"Of what?"

"My money would scare her away. You see, I, too, had humble beginnings."

He stared me straight in the eye. "I don't care who you are. There will be no marriage until she's told."

"I promise—I'll tell her the next time I see her."

Mendez let out an evil laugh. "My Maria—she has a temper. I wouldn't want to be in your shoes."

"I've loved Maria from the moment I saw her. I never intended . . ."

"I know, I know," he said, standing up. We walked to the door with his arm around my shoulder. "It's too bad in a way, I rather like you."

After Mendez left, I shook violently. He had forced the issue. I had to tell her now.

The next day, I scoured the plazas trying to find Maria an appropriate gift. I walked from barrio to barrio, preparing my speech. But I never got beyond: Maria, I have something to tell you.

That afternoon, when I returned to my office, Paco was pacing out front. When he spotted me, he ran toward me. "Juan, Juan," he said. "There's a gendarme in your office."

My heart froze. What did he want? "Good afternoon," I said to the policeman. "I'm Juan Gomez. What can I do for you?"

"Have you sold three pieces out of this collection recently?"

"I have." My brows knitted. "Why?"

"Young man," he said. "I'm here to arrest you for selling these reproductions as originals."

"But . . . they are . . ."

"You can tell your story to the captain, I have orders to bring you in." The gendarme eyed Paco and said, "Don't sell any more of these or I'll arrest you too."

"Paco," I said. "Go get my leather jacket." Maybe I could buy my freedom again.

But this officer didn't ask for anything. Inside headquarters, he escorted me to a low, partitioned area where a man sat behind an elevated wooden desk. "Captain," the gendarme said. "This is Juan Gomez—you know, the Donkey Man."

The captain looked up from his papers. "Welcome, Donkey Man," he said. "We've been expecting you."

"Can we get this mess straightened out quickly? I have work to do."

The captain smiled, his walrus mustache curling around his fat, rosy cheeks. "Don't think you're getting off this time. We've got the evidence, the witnesses . . . we're going to send you to the penal colony."

I shuddered. He thought I was guilty. "I've done nothing wrong."

"Did you sell these pieces as originals?"

"Well, yes . . . that's what the guy at the Dominguez Art Auction told me."

"You seem to have strange experiences at auctions."

"Someone delivered an invitation . . ." I paused. "I gave it to the man at the fairgrounds."

"An auction at the fairgrounds?"

"A man met me. He took me to another building where the art was displayed." I described the location. "Captain," I said. "There never was an auction, I bought the pieces at a pre-showing."

"Changing your story already?"

"I'm only trying to clarify. The auction was supposed to be July twenty-fourth, but, as far as I know, it never happened."

"Didn't you think it odd—selling original art in such a run-down place?"

"I never gave it a thought," I said. "Has an appraiser looked at them?"

"Jaime Garcia is stopping by later."

I knew him from the restaurant. He was the best in town. "I'd like to be there."

"Criminals don't get privileges." He swept his index finger into the air. "Take him away."

The gendarme locked me in a dark, dank, overcrowded cell that smelled of human waste. Several hours later, he returned. "Gomez," he said, "the captain wants to see you."

I jumped up, eager to breathe some fresher air.

The gendarme led me to a room filled with my art pieces. Jaime Garcia was plodding along like a bungler. If I hadn't known his reputation, I would have been worried. Occasionally, he oohed and aahed, which gave me hope that the gendarmes had erred.

Finally, he let his monocle fall. "Captain, these are excellent reproductions. The best I've ever seen."

My heart sank. "You sure?"

"Absolutely," he said, pointing out the determining features.

Then the captain said, "It doesn't look good, Gomez. We can't verify any of your story."

I winced. I heard the metal bars clanging shut on my freedom.

"The owner says his building's been vacant for months. If any art sale went on there, it was without his permission."

"Captain, what if I offered to buy those pieces back? Would that square things?"

"It's too late for that. We'll let a judge decide."

"A lawyer, I need a lawyer," I said, while being dragged out.

I waited and waited, but no lawyer showed up. The night slowly ticked away. I lay perfectly still with my eyes wide open. We were wall-to-wall prisoners.

Finally the guards came with breakfast—a dried-out tortilla with no water. It wasn't much, but it helped to pass the time.

The following Sunday, the newspaper carried the story of my arrest on the front page. The interview with the captain made it sound like I was guilty. At the time, I was locked away in my smelly cell, so I was unaware of the news.

Meanwhile, it was hard to tell day from night—each minute, each hour, each day passed just like the one before. I had nowhere to move. My mat doubled as my bed. The

farthest I walked was to the corner to our community bathroom—a hole in the floor.

Isolated, I had plenty of time to think. When this had happened before, at least I'd been released. And even though I lost
business, I was free to get it back. This time I was locked away
with no opportunity to clear my name. I was totally dependent on others.

Why did this have to happen now? My life was just beginning to click. I was making money and sharing it, while still
looking for new investments. I'd been helping others, too. And
most important, I was finally ready to tell Maria the truth. If
word of this got out, I'd lose her forever.

I'd just about reached the depths of despair, when one of
the guards yelled I had a visitor. I jumped up. He led me to a
room where Hector was waiting. "I just found out this morning," Hector said, his voice soft and gentle.

"Really?" Tears welled in my eyes. "I sent you a message last
Friday. I thought you deserted me."

"You know me better than that."

"I don't know what to believe. It's hell down there. I re-
quested a lawyer—no one wants my case."

"I'll bet they've cut off communication, hoping for a con-
fession."

"I told the truth. Those pieces were sold to me as originals."
I stood up and paced. "Oh God, they're going to send me to
the penal colony. I just can't spend my life in prison doing
hard labor."

Hector's eyes filled with compassion. "I'll talk to Sandoval,
my lawyer," he said. "We'll get to the bottom of this. In the
meantime, fill your mind with positive thoughts."

I stared at Hector. "I'll try. But if I don't prove my innocence this time, no one will do business with me again."

Hector called the guard. Before he left, he said, "If it helps, I
believe you're innocent."

In my cell, I tried to picture the invitation. Even if I had
read it incorrectly, the guy in the tuxedo had said each piece
was an original. The brochure! I remembered writing on it . . .

did I give that back too? In the excitement of the moment, I didn't pay attention to what I was doing. Now I was in jail. It seemed like a pretty harsh penalty.

I stretched out on my mat and closed my eyes. At least Hector was on my side. Maybe everything will work out. Soon my thoughts turned to Maria. How I longed to hold her, to see her smiling face, to listen to her gentle voice, to smell her sweet fragrance.

Suddenly, I sat up. Was that Maria? She had come to see me. Walking toward the bars, my heart leapt with joy. Then I slowed. That woman had fire in her eyes. "Maria, is that you?" I said, reaching for her hands.

She recoiled like I was poison. "I hope you've had your fun. Did you go home every Sunday, laughing about what a fool I was?"

"Maria, I . . ."

"I don't want your excuses, Donkey Man, I just couldn't believe . . ."

"Please," I interrupted. "Let me explain."

"Explain? I never want to see you again."

"Maria. *Maria.*" My arms stretched after her. "I love you."

The big door slammed. My hands pulled desperately at the iron bars. I wanted to run after her, needed to make her listen.

"What do you know, friends," one of my cellmates said. "The Donkey Man just lost his sweetie." They all laughed.

While resting my forehead against the cool bars, tears burned behind my eyes. I walked back to my mat, sat down, and hid my head between my knees. What did I expect? I should have told her. Now I felt really alone, stuck in a dreary cell with a bunch of dreary men—with nothing but a dreary life ahead of me. What made me think that I, the son of a poor tenant farmer, could make it big in the world?

Later on, Juanita came to visit. "Paco and Carlos wanted to come."

"I'm glad they didn't, although you could ask them to do me a favor." I told her about the brochure and my inability to remember what I did with it.

"They'll be happy to be doing something." Juanita paused. "It doesn't look good, does it?"

"No. Even I could believe I'm guilty." I started pacing. "Juanita, I've lost everything."

"Come on, Juan, your friends are behind you."

"Maybe—but . . . Maria, I've lost Maria."

"You mean, she deserted you while you're in jail?"

"She just found out Juan Gomez is the Donkey Man."

"You hadn't told her?" Juanita gasped. "Well . . . she'll cool down . . . eventually."

"It won't matter. By the time I get out of here, she'll have a dozen kids."

Juanita put her arm around my waist. "Juan, the truth will come out—be patient."

As the days passed and my situation remained the same, I sank to the depths of despair. Sandoval stopped in occasionally to ask me questions. He and Hector were working on my defense, but neither of them would comment on their progress. I assumed they didn't want to depress me further.

Carlos and Paco turned my office upside down, but they never found the brochure. No one corroborated my story. It appeared I was the only one who received an invitation.

Meanwhile, I wallowed in self-pity. I should have stayed a waiter, graciously accepting my tips and living a life of mediocrity. At least I'd be free instead of sitting in a locked cell, waiting for typhus while others decided my fate. I'd heard rumors about the penal colony that made my skin crawl. I was scared. I knew I'd never survive it.

The following Saturday, Hector and Sandoval came to visit. Hector's face looked drawn and pale. "What's wrong?" I said.

"They've scheduled your hearing for Monday morning."

"They can't do that. We haven't proven I'm innocent."

The young lawyer measured my gaze. For someone of Hector's stature to employ him, he had to be good. "We'll work on your testimony tomorrow. In the meantime, you better work on your attitude. The government's case is weak. So how you present yourself is going to be important."

On Sunday, my picture appeared on the front page of the paper with the heading: Donkey Man Hearing Set for Monday. And the next day, the good citizens of Mexico City packed the courtroom, anticipating my downfall.

Sandoval was about to call me to the stand, when a young man burst through the double doors. "Wait," he said. "You're holding an innocent man."

My head snapped around amid utter noise and confusion.

The judge banged his gavel. "Silence or I'll clear this courtroom."

Finally the room quieted. "Come forward, please," the judge said.

The young man approached the bench. "Your honor, my name is Santiago Perez." Then he looked at me. "I'm so sorry," he said.

My brows knitted. "Do I know you?"

"I just saw yesterday's paper."

"Señor Perez," the judge said. "Please explain yourself."

Santiago stared at me. "I hated you for a long time, Señor, we all did. My boss convinced us you were the enemy."

Again the noise. The judge banged his gavel again and again.

Sandoval took control. "Are you saying this art auction was a conspiracy to discredit my client?"

"Yes . . . he hates Señor Gomez." Santiago fidgeted. "You were taking business away—we had to stop you."

"Señor Perez," Sandoval said. "You're speaking in riddles. Why don't you start at the beginning."

"The auctions. My boss sent those men to bid up the price. He hoped the donkeys would become too expensive for you. When your business kept growing, he set up the stolen donkey bit."

"That almost did me in," I said.

"His plan backfired. The gendarmes were paid to hold you, but one got greedy and gave you your freedom. We were spreading the word around the next morning, not knowing you'd been released."

"That's how they found out at the silver mines."

"Yes." Santiago lowered his head. "I'm not proud of my part in this. When he thought you were out of business, he doubled his price. After a while, the ranchers canceled with us and gave you their business."

"Was he behind the beating?" I said.

"I know nothing of that. But he was furious when you quit attending the auctions. That's when he planned the art deal."

"Young man," Sandoval said, approaching Santiago. "Who is your boss?"

Santiago bit his lip, his eyes bouncing from me to Sandoval. Finally, he said, "Señor . . . Art . . . Trujillo."

The roar spread through the courtroom like wildfire. The judge banged his gavel repeatedly.

When the room quieted, Sandoval said, "Why would a prominent man take such a risk?"

"Greed, Señor. He used the farmers. Charged them 20 percent interest and repossessed the animals when they couldn't pay. He was the only one in business. Then Señor Gomez came along and ruined everything."

"Why are you coming forward now?" Sandoval said.

Santiago spoke to the floor. "I'm so ashamed, I didn't know until I saw the paper . . ."

Sandoval glanced at me and I shrugged.

"You see, your honor." Santiago looked at the judge. "I sat next to the Donkey Man one night at an auction. I needed a donkey, but didn't have enough money. He gave me the one he'd bought for himself."

Of course. Now I remembered.

"No one has ever . . . I . . . well, when I saw his picture, I couldn't keep it a secret."

"Case dismissed," the judge said, banging his gavel. "Somebody find Trujillo."

My first thought was Hector's words, "Lies have a way of catching up. . . ." Then Juanita, Hector, Carlos, and Paco surrounded me. "Let's celebrate," Juanita said. "I need to fatten you up."

I stood at the table feeling overwhelmed. "You're free," Hector said softly.

My face broke into a big grin. "Free," I repeated, closing my eyes. No bars, no guards, no smelly cell, no hard labor. I ran out the door and inhaled deeply. "You know something, Hector," I said. "I'm really hungry."

Becoming a Champion

Wᴇ sᴛᴀʀᴛᴇᴅ ᴡᴀʟᴋɪɴɢ ᴛᴏᴡᴀʀᴅ Pᴇᴅʀᴏ's. I twirled in the warm sunshine. Suddenly, I spotted Santiago, his head lowered, leaving the courthouse. I ran back to thank him.

"It was the only thing to do," he said.

I paused. "I guess you're out of a job."

Santiago shuffled his feet. "I'll find something."

"How about working for me?"

Santiago's face lit up. "I'm a good worker, Señor. You won't be sorry."

During the party at Pedro's, I managed to get a quiet moment with Hector. "I have only one priority now."

"Maria?" Hector said.

"I'm so afraid she's going to reject me." I sipped my tea. "She's probably found someone else."

Hector laughed. "I doubt it—not if she really loves you."

"Then there's her father," I said, running my fingers through my hair.

"Juan, just face them. It's time to get on with your life."

I squared my jaw. "Tomorrow . . . I'll do it tomorrow."

Later, Hector and I walked to my office. "I'm embarrassed Trujillo found me such an easy mark," I said. "In the future, I'm going to be more aware of my competition."

"Remember, though, in the end, Trujillo failed because he violated the basic principle of success."

"How's that?"

"Trujillo lost sight of himself, his business objectives, and competed only against you. He thought if you failed, it would make him more successful."

"Well, he almost succeeded."

"Don't get me wrong. Some competition is good . . . but overly competitive individuals tend to meet with success, only to lose it later. A champion goes out into the world to become the best *he* can be."

"A champion—I like the sound of that."

We walked into my office and I winced. The art pieces loomed in front of me like a giant monster. "I need to do something about them."

Hector sat down to catch his breath. "Nothing's stopping you from turning your mistake into something good."

"How? They're fakes."

"The whole idea of prosperity is to become a true champion by recognizing and overcoming obstacles in your environment. Always remember, true success comes solely through your own efforts."

"What do you suggest I do with these?"

"Sell them."

"What!" I said. "That's what started this whole mess."

"Look, people will still buy quality merchandise, even if they know it's an imitation."

I mulled over his words. Finally I smiled and said, "Garcia did say they're beautiful. Hector, you're a genius."

"No, I've just learned to think creatively. Creative thinkers can find a solution to every problem and a market for every thing."

"Right now, I'd almost give them away, just to get them out of my sight."

"I understand how you feel. But as a businessman, you have to accept that there are going to be times when you succeed, times when you fail, and times when you just break even." Hector sighed and looked at his watch. "You know, if I leave now, I could be home by dark."

We stood staring at each other for a long moment. "Thanks," I said, embracing him.

"Let me know what happens tomorrow."

After Hector left, I sat down to sort through two weeks' worth of messages. I had barely started when a voice said, "Señor Gomez, I've come just as you told me."

"Santiago," I said, standing up.

"What can I do, Señor?"

"I haven't thought . . ." I turned around and saw all that art staring me in the face. "Can you sell those pieces?" I said.

Santiago hesitated. "My uncle has a stall in the marketplace."

"If you can sell them, I'll pay you 10 percent commission. Sell them for more than I'm asking and we'll split the difference."

"That's very generous, Señor." Santiago walked over to the display. "Can I take ten now?"

"Under one condition," I said, helping him carry them out.

"What's that?"

"I want you to put up a big sign saying these pieces are reproductions."

Santiago laughed. "I promise."

The next day, I awoke early and headed for Maria's. The morning sun spread its eerie red glow on the mountain. I wondered if she still loved me. And, if so, would she forgive me? One thing was certain, I no longer had to hide from the truth.

When the Mendez farm came into view, my bravery left. I stopped and stared outside the gate. Finally I marched up the walk with my heart drumming in my ears.

Señora Mendez answered the door. "Dios Mio!" she said, making the sign of the cross. "I thought you were in jail."

"They freed me yesterday. I wasn't guilty. Please Señora, can I see Maria?"

"I don't know . . ." She tiptoed outside and lowered her voice. "Maria's . . ."

"Mama, who's . . . ?" Maria stopped. "You?" she said. "I told you I never wanted to see you again."

I stared at her. Her beauty took my breath away. "I can't live with that."

"Too bad, Donkey Man." She started walking away.

"I'm not leaving until you give me a chance to explain."

"I don't want to talk to you," she said, slamming the door with her foot.

Señora Mendez looked up at me and smiled. "Sometimes she's too stubborn for her own good." Then she opened the door and made a gesture for me to enter.

I found Maria sitting in the living room. Her chest was heaving. I knelt down in front of her. "What can I do to make the pain go away?"

Maria crossed her arms in front of her. "You lied to me, and I can't trust you."

"I didn't lie, I just didn't tell the whole truth."

"You used me. I hope you and your friends had a good laugh."

"That's just the problem," I said, shaking my head. "People have ideas about me that just aren't true. Look at the first time I was here—you started talking about the Donkey Man like he was some sort of god. The truth is he's just the son of a poor tenant farmer. I wanted you to fall in love with *me*—Juan Gomez—not some exaggerated reputation."

"I suppose you were just going to marry me, then tell me?"

"Truthfully, I thought about it, but your father found out."

Her eyes opened wide. "Papa knew?"

"I promised him I'd tell you the next time I saw you, but . . . I was arrested."

"No wonder he's been sticking up for you."

"Maria, I . . . my life has no meaning without you." My eyes filled with tears. "Please . . . give me another chance?"

"Well . . ."

"My name is Juan Gomez," I said, offering her my hand. "Most people know me as the Donkey Man. But please don't let that scare you away. You see, Maria Mendez, I love you. I've loved you from the first moment I saw you."

Maria uncrossed her arms and placed her hand lightly in mine. "I've . . . missed having these quiet moments alone with you."

"Then let's make it permanent. Maria, will you marry me?"

Her tears spilled over. "I love you, Juan," she whispered. "Yes, *yes*, I'll marry you."

Maria and I were married three weeks later at Hector's. After a six-week honeymoon in San Francisco, we settled into our new home in Mexico City.

During the next year, many changes occurred in my life. Santiago sold those thirty art pieces in four days by advertising them as the reproductions that put the Donkey Man behind bars. It didn't take much to realize his creative talent, so I made him a partner in the donkey business, which then grew at an even faster rate.

Juanita and the boys prospered in the restaurant business. Eventually, we remodeled Pedro's. José wanted to change from French decor to something more indigenous to Mexico. The idea worked—we became even more popular among the tourists. With José's creativity and Juanita's knack for cutting costs, our volume and our profit increased.

Manuel backed out of our business deal. He grew weary of the work; the money no longer enticed him. Since no one in his family wanted the job, Maria and I scoured the markets looking for a replacement. We found several and offered them partnerships.

The idea worked so well that any new investments I made were based on a fifty-fifty split. I found that my new partners were more involved because they were part-owners and the whole venture took less of my time.

Because the contract with the U.S. Cavalry was extended for another year and the apple orchard was slow in producing, I traveled to San Cristóbal and Veracruz every other week. I was away from my precious Maria ten days a month. This was especially difficult because we already knew she was expecting.

Our daughter, Anna, was born two months before our first anniversary. Maria almost died giving birth, so the doctor said no more children. As I'm sure you already know, Antonio, Anna, your mother, became the focus of our lives. She was a delightful baby, possessing Maria's beauty and temperament. Hector had never spent time with children and was overjoyed to become her godfather. We spent many happy weekends with him.

The Legacy Passes On

O NE TUESDAY, WHEN ANNA WAS SEVEN MONTHS old, one of Hector's servants knocked on our door late at night. "Come quickly," he said. "Señor Hector is very ill and insists on seeing you right away."

"It must be serious or Hector wouldn't send for me at such a late hour," I said to Maria.

"Go," she said. "Anna and I will meet you there tomorrow."

Riding out to the estate, I admitted to myself that Hector had been losing weight. Why couldn't life continue as it had been: Maria, Anna, Hector, and me? Now, my heart feared, it was coming to an end.

The mansion was lit up like a giant candle glowing in the black night. Were they trying to stave off the hand of death? I shuddered. "What's wrong with Hector?" I said to Miguel.

"His strength never really returned after that bout with pneumonia."

"That's impossible," I said, but his statement rang true. I had refused to see it. Hector had been protecting me. Eager to see him, I ran up the stairs. But then I stopped outside his door. I was angry because Hector's health had been kept from me, and frightened because I didn't want to lose someone I loved. Raising my fist, I knocked, praying he was still alive.

"Come in," said a voice I hardly recognized.

I took a deep breath and straightened my shoulders. It was my turn to pretend. "Hector," I said, my resolve crumbling. "Why didn't you tell me?"

Hector smiled. "Sit," he said, pointing to the edge of his bed.

My heart broke. He looked so pale, so fragile.

"I'm sorry," he said. "I'm a selfish old man. Seeing you happy made me want to stick around longer. Maria and Anna—" Hector let out a contented sigh. "They're wonderful. Thanks for sharing."

"You make it sound like a chore. We love you."

"Don't cry," Hector said, squeezing my hand. "I sent for you because we need to talk."

"Can't it wait until morning?"

"After I'm gone, you may hear this from someone else. I wanted you to understand . . ."

"But . . ."

Hector put his fingers to my lips. "Remember when I sent you off to Mexico City with the words 'opportunity is everywhere'?"

I smiled. "How could I forget?"

"If I had told you instead to share the money in your pocket, would you have listened to me?"

"Probably not." I frowned, remembering. "I was fighting to survive."

"Exactly. That's why I started teaching you how to make money."

"Why are you telling me this now?"

"Because I set you up. But the important thing to remember is you passed the test. Every success you had after that, you achieved on your own."

"You set me up? How?"

"I sent a note to Sanchez announcing your arrival. I asked him to purchase Teresa by first suggesting and explaining the financing method to you. If you didn't grasp it, then he was to try to buy the donkey outright."

"You wanted to see if I'd recognize the opportunity?"

"That . . . and how quickly you'd learn the concepts of making money. But as you know, it was your decision to part with Teresa."

"I guess I owe you a lot."

"I gave you the framework. You decided if new opportunities fit into the overall plan. And then it was you who had the courage to implement them."

My tears spilled over again. "I couldn't have done it without you."

Hector's smile lit up his pale face. "Watching you succeed has been one of the great joys of my life. I know you understand that true wealth is more than just money—it also requires spiritual and emotional wealth."

"Yes," I said, remembering my confusion over telling Maria who I was. "Unless you have all three, you can't be truly happy."

Hector placed his hand over mine. "You're like a son to me. With your knowledge, I know you'll continue my legacy of sharing. That's why I'm making you my rightful heir."

"Don't talk like this, Hector, you're going to get better."

"Not this time, son. My life is over. But I want to give you this as a constant reminder of all I've taught you."

I took the envelope and hugged him. At first he embraced me. Then I heard a rattling in his chest. Soon his arms let go and his breathing stopped. I sat there for a long time just holding him. Finally, with a wet face, I went to get the doctor. Hector Ortega—my mentor, my father, my friend—had passed on and left me his legacy.

Later that night, when I couldn't sleep, I opened the envelope Hector had given me. Inside he had listed all the lessons in the order I had learned them.

Antonio, I now pass those same papers on to you. If you learn these lessons and practice them until they become a part of your daily life, you'll prosper just as I did.

Now, my dear grandson, you know the rest of the story. After Hector died, I came here to live. Miguel stayed on as cook and I retained Sandoval because he knew so much about Hector's affairs.

Maria and Anna became the focus of my family life, while the land brought a new focus to my business life. Anna, the baby who gave Hector so much delight, grew up to become your mother. When she gave birth to you in this home, I felt a joy that I had not experienced since the time when Maria was still alive.

If I've had no other influence on your life, I hope, through my example, I've shown you how to love, respect, and share with others. I wanted you to inherit the estate, but it is only land. You now have the tools to become a truly wealthy individual.

~

Just then a loud knock on the door jolted young Antonio back to the present.

"Antonio," Anna said. "Please come down. It's time for dinner."

"I'll be there in a minute, Mother." After splashing cold water on his face, Antonio stopped again to study the picture of Juan Gomez as a young man. He smiled. The resemblance was uncanny.

When Antonio entered the banquet hall, a hush fell over the gathering. Everyone watched as he walked the length of the room. At the head of the long table, he sat down in his grandfather's chair. A little big, but comfortable.

He studied the uncertain eyes of his guests. These people received their independence today. Were they scared too? They were going to need someone to help band them together, to take their goods to market, to bargain with the railroad for the best price. Was this his first opportunity?

"I'm sorry, Antonio," Sandoval said, leaning over. "I hope you're not too disappointed that you didn't inherit the estate."

"On the contrary, Sandoval," Antonio said, smiling. "Grandpa left me something very special. He left me the keys to his true fortune."

~ Secrets of Success

by Hector Ortega

1. Opportunity is everywhere. The wise man learns to recognize and seize opportunity any time and any place it is found.

2. Cultivate patience, persistence, and self-discipline and couple them with hard work and determination.

3. Seek advice from knowledgeable people and associate with people who have goals similar to yours—people who want more from life and are willing to work for it.

4. Maintain a positive attitude, yet remain realistic in your expectations.

5. Establish a goal and focus on it until you achieve it.

6. Establish both short-term and long-term goals.

7. Establish numerous goals, yet be creative and flexible as your needs change.

8. Always have a plan in business dealings. When buying something for resale, know what you can sell it for, who your customer is—or is likely to be—and what conditions of sale are feasible.

9. Think creatively while evaluating potential opportunities.

10. Most people don't know that there are more economical ways to buy and better ways to do things, so educate yourself by learning from others and doing your own research.

11. Always have a plan—and an alternate plan to fall back on, if necessary.

12. Learn how to handle money. Don't satisfy your immediate needs or wants at the expense of your future.

13. Learn proper financial maintenance—save part of your money and budget the rest.

14. Use money wisely. Be generous yet practical, because there will always be unexpected expenses.

15. Remain open to people—do not become defensive and suspicious of everyone you meet. Remember: There are more honest people in the world than dishonest ones.

16. Do everything in life with love in your heart. Show trust in others, and they will respond by doing more for you. You will be rewarded with increasing opportunity, "luck," and success.

17. Forgiveness and compassion must always dwell in your heart. Continually fight feelings of hate, mistrust, resentment, and jealousy, because they will make you defensive and bring you down—both emotionally and financially.

18. Never take advantage of someone else's hardship or dilemma.

19. Prioritize your goals—fulfill the most important ones first.

20. Never take anything for granted. Most of the world operates in a very limited way. Sometimes you must think creatively for others in order to overcome obstacles you face together.

21. There are three types of people in the world: people who spend money, people who hoard money, and people who make money grow.

22. Keep an open mind and you'll find a world of opportunities that can offer you even greater wealth.

23. Wealth is in your mind, not in your pocket.

24. Money is nothing more than a fertilizer that can make things grow. It simply affords opportunities for a better life for yourself and others.

25. Make money grow by keeping an open mind, by taking reasonable risks, and by diversifying your investments.

26. Don't concentrate all of your energy or money into just one project.

27. In trade or in barter, sometimes you'll get more and sometimes you'll give more.

28. Become your own boss. You work hard for others; why not work hard for yourself?

29. You will never get rich working for someone else—you will just survive. By working for yourself, you take charge of your life. You determine how much you work and earn. There is no limit to what you can achieve if you have the courage to break away.

30. Never hold a grudge.
31. From understanding comes compassion.
32. All things happen for a reason. Sometimes a greater destiny, more powerful than we can understand, takes control of our lives.
33. Do what is right and profitable in business; don't let emotions rule you.
34. Share your wealth by creating opportunities for others to better themselves. If you feed a man today, he'll only starve again tomorrow. But if you can teach him how to grow his own food, he'll never starve.
35. While you should teach others how to make money, you must also show them—through example—how to share their good fortune.
36. Going out of your way to help others is the best philosophy to live by. Even though you may not be rewarded financially, the spiritual rewards are great.
37. Money is only one aspect of true wealth. If you continue to apply these lessons, spiritual wealth will naturally follow.
38. There is an order to life. As you integrate your financial and spiritual wealth, every aspect of your life will benefit.
39. Always help those people who have helped you along the way.
40. Emotional wealth encompasses a genuine respect for everything around you. It is a love of the world and of all mankind as well as a love of self.
41. Now that you know a better way, have patience with those who are less aware.
42. Foresight is the ability to accurately draw conclusions about what might happen. A successful person acquires a creative ability to see, then acts accordingly.
43. Continually add to your savings. If you don't, you can't effectively invest or help others because you won't even have enough to help yourself.
44. In your dealings, become the best you can be, without competing against others. Don't think you are better because someone else fails.

45. There is nothing stopping you from turning a mistake into an opportunity. Good things often come from what first appears to be bad.

46. Think creatively and you'll find a solution for every problem and a market for every thing.

47. In business, there will be times when you succeed, times when you fail, and times when you just break even.

48. To become a champion, you must recognize and overcome obstacles in your environment. Always remember, true success comes solely through your own efforts.

49. These lessons are the framework. You must have the wit to analyze new opportunities, decide if they fit into the overall plan, and then have the courage to implement them.

50. A genuinely wealthy person recognizes that true happiness is the ultimate goal in life. By following these lessons, one will learn to integrate financial, spiritual, and emotional wealth, thus reaching the coveted end.